SATPREM was born in 19 arrested by the Gestapo and sent to concentration camps for belonging to the French Resistance. After undergoing that ordeal, broken in his heart and soul and body, he traveled to Egypt, then to India, where he served in the government of Pondicherry, then the administrative capital of French India. There he discovered the "new evolution" envisioned by Sri Aurobindo—"Man is a transitional being"—handed in his resignation and left for the Amazon jungle, ever in search of the "true adventure."

Upon his return to India in 1953, at the age of thirty, he became a mendicant Sannyasi, practiced Tantrism, finally to abandon all these paths to put himself at the service of Mother and Sri Aurobindo, to whom he dedicated his first nonfiction work, *Sri Aurobindo or the Adventure of Consciousness,* then a second nonfiction work, *On the Way to Supermanhood.* He stayed beside Mother for 19 years, becoming her confidant and witness, and collecting numerous personal conversations that form *Mother's Agenda.* This adventure with her who was seeking the secret of the transition to the next species gave rise to a trilogy on Mother (*The Divine Materialism, The New Species, The Mutation of Death*), then to a fable, *Gringo,* and finally to *The Mind of the Cells,* his latest nonfiction work, which distills the essence of Mother's discovery: a change in the genetic program and a different view of death. Satprem now lives withdrawn from public life to devote himself to Mother's work and the transition in the consciousness of the body.

LUC VENET, who wrote the commentary of this book and interviewed Satprem, is a long-time friend and collaborator. He left a career in mathematics to dedicate himself to another "science" with more bearing on the deeper mechanisms of life and evolution and the possibilities of transforming the human species. He heads the New York-based Institute for Evolutionary Research, which is devoted to promoting the evolutionary experience of Mother and Sri Aurobindo in the United States.

LIFE

WITHOUT DEATH

ALSO BY SATPREM

Sri Aurobindo or
The Adventure of Consciousness (1984)
By the Body of the Earth (1978)
*

Mother:
1. *The Divine Materialism* (1986)
2. *The New Species* (1982)
3. *The Mutation of Death* (1987)
*

The Mind of the Cells (1982)
On the Way to Supermanhood (1986)

Mother's Agenda
1951-1973
13 volumes

Recorded by Satprem in the course of numerous personal conversations with Mother, the complete logbook of her fabulous exploration in the cellular consciousness of the human body. Twenty-three years of experiences which parallel some of the most recent theories of modern physics. Perhaps the key to man's passage to the next species. (Vols. 1, 2, 3, 4, 5, 12 & 13 published in English)

LIFE

WITHOUT DEATH

SATPREM ☆ LUC VENET

Translated from the French

Institute for Evolutionary Research
200 Park Avenue, New York, N.Y. 10166

Library of Congress Cataloging-in-Publication Data

Satprem, 1923-
    Life without death.

    Translation of: Vie sans mort.
    Bibliography: p.
    1. Spiritual life. 2. Life--Miscellanea.
I. Venet, Luc. II. Title.
BL624.S26413   1988   294.5'42   88-8870
ISBN 0-938710-23-0

CONTENTS

Death must be overcome;
there must be no more death.
This is very clear.

MOTHER

It isn't for cancer
that we must find a cure;
it's for death.

SATPREM

Introduction

THE WORLD is about to change—but perhaps not as we may imagine. In fact, somewhere, the change is already accomplished. There only remains to implement it fully, in broad daylight. The goal of this short book is to try to explain the specific conditions of this change, how it can take place and is already taking place. In it will not be found any methods, formulas or speculations on the state of the future world, only certain patent human truths that each one can use as he pleases.

The change in question here is not external, mechanical or scientific, but internal and human. It is the human world that must change—or perhaps simply the way we see and feel and manipulate our world. It is a question of implementing another way of living on earth, a being after man as radically different from us as we may be from our ancestor, the ape. If such a being is to see the light of day on this earth, the evolutionary wisdom and simplicity will produce it *from us*, from what we are today, and not out of some mystical and misty heaven, or out of a proliferation of computers—there must exist a link between it and us. Thus, if we observe and study what we are without human complacency, with scientific honesty, we could say, we ought to be able to find *in ourselves* a key, a means for making that transition, or at least for taking a few steps on the road that leads to the future of our species.

1

This great adventure into the unknown future was begun by Sri Aurobindo more than seventy years ago. Methodically, using himself as a subject of experiment, he went down one by one through the various levels of his being, of his own human substance, what we usually call "ourselves" in such a simple and natural way that we never really pay attention to it. Sri Aurobindo paid a lot of attention, studied minutely, going down farther and farther, to the extreme limit, to the body's material foundation, what sets the cells in motion, in order to understand how a human being really functions. "I have been testing day and night for years upon years more scrupulously than any scientist his theory or his method on the physical plane," he would say. And what does set the human cells in motion? What is the real mechanism? Later, Mother, his companion, followed him there. She, too, went all the way down into the dangerous and fantastic realm that holds the secrets of the functioning of the human body. That "descent" into one's own being is the whole difficulty and the key to the transition we are seeking. Their experiential observations, their discoveries are of considerable interest for whoever is concerned with the future. Indeed, they found the link, the connection in us that can open the door to the next being. Alas, man's nature is such that for the most part he wants easy formulas, "gimmicks" to ameliorate everyday life. The few disciples that Sri Aurobindo had gathered around himself in order to spread the fruit of his discoveries in humanity at large found it more convenient to make him into a god, then, after his departure in 1950, to inflict the same fate on Mother. "Why do men want to worship!" exclaimed Mother. "It is far better to *become* than to worship. It's laziness that makes one worship." Thus, hardly anyone around Mother and Sri Aurobindo really understood that their discovery in the cellular consciousness of a human body was the key to an *effective* change to another state. One had, naturally, to be willing to question one's own makeup, to be willing to leave an old, uncomfortable skin for another that one did not know—one cannot reasonably expect to go toward the new while prudently clinging to the old. Failing to use Sri Aurobindo's wonderful discoveries on oneself, as an evolutionary leaven, it was no doubt easier to empty them of their universal content by reducing them to a dogma, and trying to make a new religion out of them.

Fortunately, there was a grace that did not let this happen. Indeed, we scarcely need another religion. What we need is to give meaning to our present life on earth, to comprehend our real position and where we are going as a species. We do not need more incense but more sense. If we could open, however slightly, the true door of our future, our present would appear singularly lighter; we would perhaps understand what we are going through and the meaning of the disconcerting chaos that seems to rule over present life on earth.

Thus, by sheer luck, Mother was able to find a man who understood her, what she was trying to do. To "understand," in this case, did not just mean adhering in principle to the idea of a terrestrial transformation, not just raising it to the status of a personal ideal that one wears everywhere like a necktie, the way disciples tend to do; to understand meant to begin to feel in one's own flesh the first tremors of something new and rather frightening; it meant bringing to light certain deep-seated quirks buried in one's depths, not always pleasant or "divine"; it meant accepting, every minute of the day, to leave a solid and concrete present for a mysterious and intangible future—it meant going against all common sense. One had to be a little crazy—or truly athirst for something else. Years later, Mother said to Satprem,

"When I first saw you, it was . . . you know, like something saying, 'That one.'" With Mother there was no need for many words or explanations; it was mainly facts that interested her.

At any rate, that *one* being understood and was ready to embark on the unknown with her is invaluable to us, left as we are with the human burden. Perhaps the secrets that Mother discovered in the depths of the cells of her body can be of use to us, in our daily life, and perhaps they can also be useful to the collective life of the planet? After Mother left her body in 1973, these secrets had to *live* somewhere, to be active somewhere—and not just sterilely consigned to some new Tables of the Law. One man had to open his heart and flesh to keep the little flame alive. A human body was needed to house that Fire. Let us rejoice, for the Fire is burning somewhere on this earth; nothing is lost. Whether that man is registered at City Hall under one name or another, whether he was born in France (like Mother) and dresses in Western clothes or not is rather unimportant. He is the Keeper of the Flame; that is the important point—the following pages will show it abundantly. When he can share the secrets that drive him with his fellow human beings, the face of this earth will change; it will be a brand-new earth—or perhaps simply the liberation of the old one. But that depends a little on us, too.

LET US again emphasize that there can be no ready-made answers or formulas when it comes to what impels human life on earth. Each life is different and unique—and it is good that it should be so. The following texts evoke the extraordinary experience begun by Sri Aurobindo, continued and enlarged by Mother, and em-

4

bodied by a human brother named Satprem. These texts do not pretend to set forth the human Truth once and for all; the vocabulary and words used could be entirely different without the experience's being in the least affected. What matters is the experience itself and its inherent power to change life on earth. Each person therefore can draw from these texts as he wishes—and maybe uncover a clue for his own life. After all, the human cell is identical in each human being. Through it, the Catholic peasant of the Andes is unknowingly in communion with the Hindu intellectual from Banaras. And since we do not always speak the same language, our cells will perhaps be able to sort things out more easily and simply than our heads. Finally, it is entirely possible that similar experiences are taking place in other points of the globe, in other climates and other languages, for, as we shall see, what matters is not so much our "belief" in this or that as our CRY.

L. V.

PART ONE

SRI AUROBINDO

The Door Is Open

SRI AUROBINDO'S life was in many respects exemplary. The first part—until he was about forty—was filled with all that an ordinary human life can be filled with, and somewhat more.[1] The second part—from 1910 to 1950—was spent entirely in Pondicherry and disappears into a deep well of silence of which nothing can apparently be fathomed. Yet it is this second part of Sri Aurobindo's life that is of interest to us, what took place in that silent room on the second floor of the Ashram building, as he sat alone in his big armchair with imposing armrests, gazing at the wall in front of him. What battles was he waging in an invisible reality which yet molds our lives? What depths was he probing in a being that had long ceased to incarnate a small individual periphery? What Hope of new life was his love drawing down here?

If we understand what he was doing, understand that *everything* in this material world is set in motion by its invisible, "subtle" counterpart—its archetype on the other side of the mirror, we could say—then we understand that it is enough to act on that other side, in that other "dimension," in order to produce an effective result here; and, above all, we understand that *no* material action here can ever be ef-

---

1. See biographical notes at the end of this book.

fective and lasting unless the other one, "elsewhere," has occurred—nothing really changes unless it changes *there*.

(*Sri Aurobindo:*) When I speak of the resistance of the material world, I do not mean the external material world but the subtle material. There is the subtle and the external material, and when I say that Matter is impenetrable, I mean that the subtle-material has not accepted the Truth. (33:508)

Thus, Sri Aurobindo's "withdrawal" was hardly a withdrawal at all. He was merely working in the only substance that really matters, the one that holds the power to change life. Therefore, we will constantly need to "adjust" ourselves to this entirely different perception of reality in order to follow Sri Aurobindo; we will have to use intuition as a first step toward a fuller and more concrete understanding, jump over our fine reason, whose range of action is all too limited. After all, if our goal is to change things in their foundation, we must use the appropriate means. The reason and its rigid laws have their usefulness for manipulating and operating on our external world, but if we want to change the laws, we must go down to the root of the laws.

The Earth

The danger of these "invisible" worlds, of course, is that they are extremely attractive. They are much vaster and richer than the superficial world we live in, made of an infinitely supple substance, and, above all, they hold a *real* power of action when we know how to act there. In and for themselves, therefore, they exert a powerful attraction to which many have succumbed. In their infinite and eternal perspective, our poor, temporal, and clumsy earth cuts a rather diminutive figure. Let this small and imperfect sphere drift wherever it may—what does it matter!—we are anchored in a boundless and eternal substance, forever free of earthly upheavals.

Unfortunately, this attitude inevitably leads to one small contradiction: Why be born in a body made of earthly matter if it is simply to forsake the earth and live in the clouds? There may be a reason for our birth in a body made of material atoms and material cells. And maybe nothing will ever be really fulfilled, happy and *one*—even "up above"—so long as this question has not found an integral and harmonious and *material* answer?

Thus, from the start, Sri Aurobindo puts us on notice:

I am concerned with the earth, not with worlds beyond for their own sake; it is a terrestrial realisation that I seek and not a flight to distant summits. (26:124)

And so does Mother:

That's always a possibility—to escape by going elsewhere. Many people have done it. They have gone elsewhere, into another, more or less subtle world. You see, there are millions of ways of escaping; there's only one way of staying, which is to have real courage and endurance, to accept all the appearance of infirmity, powerlessness, incomprehension—the appearance of, yes, a negation of the Truth. But if one does not accept

11

that, things will never change! As for those who want to remain great, luminous, strong, powerful, and so on and so forth, well, let them—they can do nothing for the earth. (9/25/65)[1]

And this:

(Mother:) At times, one gets the feeling that there is an extraordinary secret to discover, and it's right there, almost at one's fingertips, and one is about to catch the Thing, to know. . . . Sometimes, for a second, one catches a glimpse of the Secret; there's an opening, and then it closes up again. Then, again, the veil is removed for a second, and one knows a little more. Yesterday the Secret was right there, completely clear, completely open. . . . And, well, I saw that secret; I saw that it is in earthly matter, on earth, that the Supreme becomes perfect. (6/5/60)

Reason

Hence the earth is our real focus of interest. It is a *physical* solution to the problem of the world that we seek. But our means of attaining it will be spiritual, directed inwardly,

---

1. Mother's quotations in this book are drawn from *MOTHER'S AGENDA* in 13 volumes. The reference indicates the date of Mother's particular conversation with Satprem (September 25, 1965, in the present case). Sri Aurobindo's quotations are taken mostly from the Centenary Edition. The reference indicates the volume and the page number (see list of volumes at the end of the book).

for they alone can touch the deeper causes of things, the true springs of the mechanism of life.

(Sri Aurobindo:) **The error of the practical reason is an excessive subjection to the apparent fact which it can immediately feel as real and an insufficient courage in carrying profounder facts of potentiality to their logical conclusion. What is, is the realisation of an anterior potentiality; present potentiality is a clue to future realisation. And here potentiality exists; for the mastery of phenomena depends upon a knowledge of their causes and processes and if we know the causes of error, sorrow, pain, death, we may labour with some hope towards their elimination. For knowledge is power and mastery. In fact, we do pursue as an ideal, so far as we may, the elimination of all these negative or adverse phenomena. We seek constantly to minimise the causes of error, pain and suffering. Science, as its knowledge increases, dreams of regulating birth and of indefinitely prolonging life, if not of effecting the entire conquest of death. But because we envisage only external or secondary causes, we can only think of removing them to a distance and not of eliminating the actual roots of that against which we struggle. And we are thus limited because we strive towards secondary perceptions and not towards root-knowledge, because we know processes of things, but not their essence. We thus arrive at a more powerful manipulation of circumstances, but not at essential control. But if we**

could grasp the essential nature and the essential cause of error, suffering and death, we might hope to arrive at a mastery over them which should be not relative but entire. We might hope even to eliminate them altogether and justify the dominant instinct of our nature by the conquest of that absolute good, bliss, knowledge and immortality which our intuitions perceive as the true and ultimate condition of the human being. (18:56)

It is hardly necessary, today, to dwell on the ambiguity of science's "blessings," which always seem to embody the very opposite of their quality, like a seed of death at the core. Perhaps the real problem of science is its awesome effectiveness—if it were not so extraordinarily effective, the human race would have toppled it long ago and discovered the Reality it conceals so well.

(Sri Aurobindo:) **Everybody knows that Science is not a statement of the truth of things, but only a language expressing a certain experience of objects, their structure, their mathematics, a coordinated and utilisable impression of their processes—it is nothing more. Matter itself is something (a formation of energy perhaps?) of which we know superficially the structure as it appears to our mind and senses and to certain examining instruments (about which it is now suspected that they largely determine their own results, Nature adapting its replies to the instrument used) but more than that no scientist knows and can know. (22:368)**

14

Man

Let us therefore embark with Sri Aurobindo and Mother, leaving all our reasonable baggage behind. A new species on earth is not something reasonable. And why not? Are we so foolish to envision a being after man? Has not Darwin shown that species evolve, that one species is born from another? Why should it be different for man?

(Sri Aurobindo:) Because man is a mental being, he naturally imagines that mind is the one great leader and actor and creator or the indispensable agent in the universe. But this is an error; even for knowledge mind is not the only or the greatest possible instrument, the one aspirant and discoverer. Mind is a clumsy interlude between Nature's vast and precise subconscient action and the vaster infallible superconscient action of the Godhead. There is nothing mind can do that cannot be better done in the mind's immobility and thought-free stillness. (17:11)

The truth is that man is nothing, or not much, but he can *become*—a great destiny is his if he only consents to have a fairer idea of himself and of the true place he occupies in the universe.

(Sri Aurobindo:) Man in himself is little more than an ambitious nothing. He is a littleness that reaches to a wideness and a grandeur that are beyond him, a dwarf enamoured of the heights. His mind is a dark ray in the splendours of the universal Mind. His life is a striving, exulting,

15

suffering, an eager passion-tossed and sorrow-stricken or a blindly and dumbly longing petty moment of the universal Life. His body is a labouring perishable speck in the material universe. This cannot be the end of the mysterious upward surge of Nature. There is something beyond, something that mankind shall be; it is seen now only in broken glimpses through rifts in the great wall of limitations that deny its possibility and existence. An immortal soul is somewhere within him and gives out some sparks of its presence; above an eternal spirit overshadows him and upholds the soul-continuity of his nature. But this greater spirit is obstructed from descent by the hard lid of his constructed personality; and that inner luminous soul is wrapped, stifled, oppressed in dense outer coatings. . . .

Man's greatness is not in what he is, but in what he makes possible. His glory is that he is the closed space and secret workshop of a living labour in which supermanhood is being made ready by a divine Craftsman. But he is admitted too to a yet greater greatness and it is this that, allowed to be unlike the lower creation, he is partly an artisan of this divine change; his conscious assent, his consecrated will and participation are needed that into his body may descend the glory that will replace him. (17:8)

And Sri Aurobindo adds:

**Man is a transitional being; he is not final. . . .
The step from man to superman is the next approaching achievement in the earth's evolution.
It is inevitable because it is at once the intention
of the inner Spirit and the logic of Nature's
process. (17:7)**

The Mental Principle

This new principle of consciousness that is to use the
human receptacle to incarnate itself was called the *Supermind* or *Supramental* by Sri Aurobindo. It is the supramental consciousness that is to replace the mental consciousness
of present man. And as this new principle of consciousness
becomes active within the earthly body (that is, as it actually touches earthly matter), it will devise its own means of
expression, its own forms and organs from the ones that
exist at present—it will perform evolution, much as the introduction of the mental principle a few million years ago
determined the form and conditions of the man we know
today. Sri Aurobindo's fantastic labor was to open the door
to the possibility of this new consciousness, to "draw" it down
here.

(Sri Aurobindo:) **I am at present engaged in
bringing the Supermind into the physical consciousness, down even to the sub-material. The
physical is by nature inert and does not want to
be rendered conscient. It offers much greater resistance as it is unwilling to change. One feels as
if "digging the earth," as the Veda says. It is lit-**

17

erally digging from Supermind above to Supermind below. (33:298)

The descent of the supramental means only that the Power will be there in the earth-consciousness as a living force just as the thinking mental and higher mental are already there. (26:146)

If I feel practically certain of the supramental Descent (I do not fix a date), it is because I have my grounds for the belief, not a faith in the air. I know that the supramental Descent is inevitable—I have faith in view of my experience that the time can be and should be now and not in a later age. (26:469)

Everything is, of course, always "there," since the beginning of time, in a state of potentiality; if it were not already there as a principle, it could never become reality. Things cannot spring from nothing—but they do have to accept to show their face. How does one make the Supermind, a new principle of consciousness, show its face on earth? To give it a name is not enough. How does one "activate" a principle still dormant, a new, *supra*-mental determinism on an earth entirely dominated by a self-contained mental determinism? One is at a loss to contemplate what it means really to open a door that does not exist anywhere as a reality. This is nothing short of creation.

But clearly, the first step is for that mental determinism to cease being. In order for the new principle to take its place, the old one must stop being wholly determinant on earth. Sri Aurobindo, therefore, set out in a methodical and conscientious search, in himself at first, of everything that was "determined" or conditioned by the mental activity in our human nature.

Man's usual conception on this subject is that his entire mental activity is limited to his thinking intelligence—his capacity to think things out—and to a few automatic (hence unimportant) nervous reactions and "reflexes" that drive his heart, lungs, digestive functions, etc., and constitute the rest of his sentient and nervous self. Based on this very scanty picture, the spiritual teachings of all ages have urged us to strive for "mental silence"—to stop the higher mental activity, the thought process—so we may enter the "Kingdom of God," "Liberation," "Nirvana," or God knows what. And that is absolutely true, those teachings are absolutely right: to stop thoughts is a wonderful, refreshing bath, a kind of "liberation" indeed; to be able to stop at will the racket that goes on upstairs night and day is an immense—if partial—liberation.

Unfortunately, that does not really solve the problem. Once this first result has been achieved, we begin to perceive, with dizzying precision, a whole unruly mass of "mentally coated" activities in ourselves: emotions, sentiments, reactions to the stimuli of daily life, and even bodily reflexes, such as sensations of cold, heat, hunger, pain, joy, attraction, revulsion, fatigue, restlessness—a whole teeming world with its own laws, its own life, upon which thought (or the stopping of thoughts) has no effect whatsoever. In short, although we may like to think otherwise, mastery of the thought process does not qualify us for leaving the good, everyday humanity. To leave it, or simply get to the bottom of it, we must obviously go further—or deeper.

Spirituality

Confronted by this major obstacle, which constantly threatened the solidity and permanence of a painfully acquired realization, the spiritualists found only one answer: to protect their realization behind high walls, to cut themselves off from a life rather too prone to arouse in man the kind of reactions contrary to the ideal pursued. In a monastery, in the Himalayas, one can "devote oneself to God" to one's heart's content, give oneself exclusively to the object of one's search without the constant nagging and embarrassment of ordinary life.

(Mother:) **Of course, one understands why the saints, the sages, those who wanted to feel themselves constantly in that divine atmosphere, had removed all material things from their life—because they were not transformed, and so they kept slipping back into the other way of being, and that can become quite . . . unpleasant at times. But to transform this material life . . . is INCOMPARABLY, immensely superior, in the sense that it gives an extraordinary STABILITY, consciousness and REALITY. (9/30/67)**

(Sri Aurobindo:) **The spiritual change begins by an influence of the inner being and the higher spiritual mind, an action felt and accepted on the surface; but this by itself can lead only to an illumined mental idealism or to the growth of a religious mind, a religious temperament and some devotion in the heart and piety in the conduct; it is a first approach of mind to spirit, but**

it cannot make a radical change: more has to be done, we have to live deeper within, we have to exceed our present consciousness and surpass our present status of Nature. (19:722)

The earth-law has to be changed and a new atmosphere has to be created. The question is not merely to have knowledge, power, etc., but to bring it down, the whole difficulty is to make it flow down. (33:148)

(Mother:) When you are on the ascending path, the work is relatively easy. I had already covered that path at the beginning of the century and established a conscious relationship with the Supreme—with "That" which is beyond the Personal and the gods and all external expressions of the Divine, but also beyond the Absolute Impersonal. It is something one cannot speak of; one must experience it. And "that" is what must be brought down into matter. This is the descending path, the one I began with Sri Aurobindo, and there the work is immense. (5/19/59)

The Body

Life can only change if we concern ourselves with life. The animal body can only change if we resolve to probe it. When do we stop, even for a minute, to ask our body how it is doing, or simply give a little sign of friendly recognition? We walk

21

with it, sleep with it, cut firewood with it—well, it's so natural, you see; it just works!

(Sri Aurobindo:) **In the past the body was regarded by spiritual seekers rather as an obstacle, as something to be overcome and discarded, than as an instrument of spiritual perfection and a field of the spiritual change. It has been condemned as a grossness of Matter, as an insuperable impediment and the limitations of the body as something unchangeable making transformation impossible. This is because the human body even at its best seems only to be driven by an energy of life which has its own limits and is debased in its smaller physical activities by much that is petty or coarse or evil, the body in itself is burdened with the inertia and inconscience of Matter, only partly awake and, although quickened and animated by a nervous activity, subconscient in the fundamental action of its constituent cells and tissues and their secret workings. (16:7)**

The importance of the body is obvious; it is because he has developed or been given a body and brain capable of receiving and serving a progressive mental illumination that man has risen above the animal. Equally, it can only be by developing a body or at least a functioning of the physical instrument capable of receiving and serving a still higher illumination that he will rise above himself and realise, not merely in thought and in his internal being but in life, a

perfectly divine manhood. Otherwise either the
promise of Life is canceled, its meaning annulled and earthly being can only realise
Sachchidananda [the Eternal] by abolishing itself, by shedding from it mind, life and body and
returning to the pure Infinite, or else man is not
the divine instrument, there is a destined limit
to the consciously progressive power which dis-
tinguishes him from all other terrestrial exist-
ences and as he has replaced them in the front
of things, so another must eventually replace
him and assume his heritage. (18:231)

The Future

Let us therefore get out of our monasteries and privileged
islands to seize total life where it is: in the street, at the of-
fice, and wherever our body lives, walks, and breathes. Life
is not contradictory; it just is. It is up to us to understand
and integrate it. The body, our body, is the site of the battle
of the next species. It is the evolutionary crucible in which
God wants to work out Man. Sri Aurobindo tells us—proves
through his own example—that we can participate in and
even hasten the movement. We are invited to participate in
our own future.

(Sri Aurobindo:) Man as he is cannot be the last
term of that evolution: he is too imperfect an expression of the Spirit, mind itself a too limited
form and instrumentation, mind is only a middle
term of consciousness, the mental being can
only be a transitional being. If, then, man is in-

capable of exceeding mentality, he must be surpassed and Supermind and superman must manifest and take the lead of the creation. But if his mind is capable of opening to what exceeds it, then there is no more reason why man himself should not arrive at Supermind and supermanhood or at least lend his mentality, life and body to an evolution of that greater term of the Spirit manifesting in Nature. (19:846)

Will we decline the invitation? It would be a pity, especially for us, for everything moves on and progresses constantly in this universe; what stands still must die and fall back to dust.

(Sri Aurobindo:) **Otherwise what will be ultimately accomplished is an achievement by the few initiating a new order of beings, while humanity will have passed sentence of unfitness on itself and may fall back into an evolutionary decline or a stationary immobility; for it is the constant upward effort that has kept humanity alive and maintained for it its place in the front of creation. (19:724)**

But because the burden which is being laid on mankind is too great for the present littleness of the human personality and its petty mind and small life-instincts, because it cannot operate the needed change, because it is using this new apparatus and organisation to serve the old infraspiritual and infrarational life-self of humanity, the destiny of the race seems to be heading

dangerously, as if impatiently and in spite of itself, under the drive of the vital ego seized by colossal forces which are on the same scale as the huge mechanical organisation of life and scientific knowledge which it has evolved, a scale too large for its reason and will to handle, into a prolonged confusion and perilous crisis and darkness of violent shifting incertitude. Even if it turns out to be a passing phase or appearance and a tolerable structural accommodation is found which will enable mankind to proceed less catastrophically on its uncertain journey, this can only be a respite. For the problem is fundamental and in putting it evolutionary Nature in man is confronting herself with a critical choice which must one day be solved in the true sense if the race is to arrive or even to survive. (19:1055)

Matter

Fabulous possibilities are open before us. A marvelous future, full of surprises and joy, is awaiting us if we know how to grasp the right thread of our evolution and have the courage to look at ourselves objectively.

To begin with, our own matter, our body, *already* contains every miracle and every marvel in a dormant state, as it were—we must "awaken" or un-cover them, put them in contact with their solar counterpart above: we must join the Divine below with the Divine above.

(Sri Aurobindo:) Matter, the medium of all this evolution, is seemingly inconscient and inanimate; but it appears to us so only because we are unable to sense consciousness outside a certain limited range, a fixed scale or gamut to which we have access. Below us there are lower ranges to which we are insensible and these we call subconscience or inconscience. Above us are higher ranges which are, to our inferior nature, an unseizable superconscience. The difficulty of Matter is not an absolute inconscience, but an obscured consciousness limited by its own movement—vaguely, dumbly, blindly self-aware, not really responsive to anything outside its own form and forces. At its worst it can be called not so much inconscience as nescience. The awakening of a greater and yet greater consciousness in this Nescience is the miracle of the universe of Matter. . . . In every particle, atom, molecule, cell of Matter there lives hidden and works unknown all the omniscience of the Eternal and all the omnipotence of the Infinite. (17:14)

Involution of a superconscient Spirit in inconscient Matter is the secret of this visible and apparent world and the evolution of this Superconscient out of inconscient Nature is the keyword of the earth's riddle. Earth-life is the self-chosen habitation of a great Divinity and his aeonic will is to change it from a blind prison into his splendid mansion and high heaven-reaching temple.

... The long process of terrestrial formation and

26

creation, the ambiguous miracle of life, the struggle of mind to appear and grow in an apparent vast Ignorance and to reign there as interpreter and creator and master, the intimations of a greater something that passes beyond the finite marvel of Mind to the infinite marvels of the Spirit, are not a meaningless and fortuitous passing result of some cosmic Chance with its huge combination of coincidences; they are not the lucky play of some blind material Force. These things are and can be only because of something eternal and divine that concealed itself in energy and form of Matter. The secret of the terrestrial evolution is the slow and progressive liberation of this latent indwelling spirit, the difficult appearance of Something or Someone already involved with all its potential forces in a first formal basis of supporting substance, its greater slowly emerging movements locked up in an initial expressive power of Matter.

... Because this infinite Spirit and eternal Divinity is here concealed in the process of material Nature, the evolution of a power beyond Mind is not only possible, but inevitable. If all were result of cosmic Chance there need be no necessity of its appearance, even as there was no necessity for any embarrassing emergence of a stumbling and striving vital consciousness in the mechanical whirl of Matter. And if all were the works of a mechanical Force, then too mind need not have unexpectedly appeared as a superior mechanism labouring to deal with Nature's grosser first machine and supermind would be

**still more a superfluity and a luminous inso-
lence. Or, if a limited experimenting external
Creator were the inventor of this universe, there
would be no reason why he should not stop short
at mind, content with the ingenuity of his
labour. But since the Divinity is involved here
and is emerging, it is inevitable that all his
powers or degrees of power should emerge one
after the other till the whole glory is embodied
and visible. (17:17-20)**

The Layers of Being

Hence, the work of the pioneer is to start "digging" in the
various layers of his being in order to put them in contact
one by one with Peace, Light, Joy—the pure air of the surface. First, he "digs" in everything that is intellectual mental activity in himself; then, in the emotional layers, the
desires and emotional reactions of all kinds (what Mother
and Sri Aurobindo called the vital); then, in an unbelievable throng of tiny corporeal reactions, which are so "natural" and automatic that we never pay attention to them,
despite the fact that they are the very stuff of our daily
physical existence: "I must go down the stairs slowly or I
may fall." "See this crease in the carpet there right in front
of me? Just perfect to trip and break a leg!" "If I climb the
hill too fast, I'll be out of breath; if I make too many appoint-
ments, I'll get tired; if I stay more than an hour in the sun,
I'll resemble a lobster." And on and on, ad nauseam. Almost
nothing in our life is spontaneous; everything is as if per-
ceived in advance and "authorized" or not by a fear-ridden
and droning dwarf, hidden somewhere inside our being. Its

action is so polished, so "natural," that we end up making no distinction between it and us. Whether we like it or not, it becomes our mouthpiece and the trusted guide for every action in our life. Even catching it in the act is not enough to challenge its authority. This dwarf is what Mother called "the physical mind."

(Mother:) **All these last few days, I have been confronting a problem as old as the world and which has become extremely acute. It was, in the most material physical consciousness, what Sri Aurobindo calls "disbelief"—it isn't doubt (doubt belongs mostly to the mind). It's almost the refusal to accept what is obvious the moment it isn't part of the little everyday routine of ordinary sensations and reactions: a sort of incapacity to accept and acknowledge the exceptional. This disbelief is the basis of our consciousness. And it comes with . . . (we call it "thought," but that's a big word for quite an ordinary thing) a physical-mental activity that produces a "thought" and always foresees, imagines or concludes (depending on the case) in a way that I personally call** *defeatist.* **That is to say, it automatically brings in the idea of all the bad things that can happen. And this in the most commonplace domain, the most ordinary, narrow and banal life, such as eating, moving, etc. Really the most vulgar things. Where thought is concerned, it is fairly easy to resolve and control, but those reactions which come from all the way down . . . It's so tiny one can hardly express it to oneself. (12/13/60)**

The Subconscious

Then the pioneer enters a dark zone, full of dangers and risks and as vast as an ocean, a bottomless swamp, the real difficulty of the physical transformation to another species: the subconscious.

(Sri Aurobindo:) **You have to go on working and working year after year, point after point, till you come to a central point in the subconscient which has to be conquered and it is the crux of the whole problem, hence exceedingly difficult. ... This point in the subconscient is the seed and it goes on sprouting and sprouting till you have cut out the seed. (36:180)**

There are no lights there, no higher illuminations, no Divine. Everybody is equal, without noticeable difference— the Christian and the Buddhist and the man without religion—both feet firmly stuck in mud. It is an indescribable place because it contains *everything*. It is our base, the ground on which the human species has grown millennium after millennium. It is millions of years old and we all have the dubious privilege of plunging our roots into it, adding our personal contribution to it life after life. Twenty-four hours a day it meticulously records, in its own language, our every gesture and action, conscious or unconscious. We visit there almost every night, during our sleep, and do not retain any recollection of our visits.

(Sri Aurobindo:) **It contains all the reactions to life which struggle out as a slowly evolving and self-formulating consciousness, but it contains**

them not as ideas or perceptions or conscious reactions but as the blind substance of these things. Also all that is consciously experienced sinks down into the subconscient not as experience but as obscure and obstinate impressions of experience and can come up at any time as dreams, as mechanical repetitions of past thought, feeling, action, etc., as "complexes" exploding into action and event etc., etc. The subconscient is the main cause why all things repeat themselves and nothing ever gets changed except in appearances. It is the cause why, people say, character cannot be changed, also of the constant return of things one hoped to have got rid of. All seeds are there and all the sanskaras [imprints] of the mind and vital and body,—it is the main support of death and disease and the last fortress (seemingly impregnable) of the Ignorance. All that is suppressed without being wholly got rid of sinks down there and remains in seed ready to surge up or sprout up at any moment. (32:247)

(Mother:) I am right in the subconscious—a subconscious, oh, hopelessly riddled with weakness, dullness and . . . (what shall I say?) enslaved by a host of things—enslaved by EVERYTHING. Oh, night after night, night after night, it unfolds before me, to show me. Last night it was indescribable! And it goes on and on; it seems limitless. So, naturally, the body feels the effects, poor thing! That's its subconscious, not personal—it's personal and not per-

sonal: it becomes personal when it enters the
body. You can't imagine the accumulation of impressions that are recorded and stored there,
one on top of another. Outwardly, you haven't
even noticed anything—the waking consciousness doesn't even notice them, but they keep
entering, piling up on top of one another—
horrible! (2/18/61)

No real freedom is possible so long as "that" exists and
controls life, no divine species on earth and no hope of transformation. A new man means new roots and a new base. It
is a complete illusion—the illusion of all spiritual teachings—to call for a New Earth and a New Man while mod-
estly averting one's eyes from that impossible quagmire.
(One can understand the reluctance of these spiritual teachings, but then one can also understand why nothing has ever
really changed on earth and in man since the advent of the
great human religions: They have always prudently skirted
the real issue.)

(Sri Aurobindo:) **It is a Herculean labour, for,
when one enters there, it is a sort of unexplored
continent. Previous Yogis came down to the
vital. If I had been made to see it before, probably I would have been less enthusiastic.** (31:196)

The truth is, we have to go down there, too, and overcome.
That is the true labor and the marvel of Mother and Sri
Aurobindo.

(Sri Aurobindo:) **As for the Mother and myself,
we have had to try all ways, follow all methods,**

to surmount mountains of difficulties, a far heavier burden to bear than you or anybody else in the Ashram or outside, far more difficult conditions, battles to fight, wounds to endure, ways to cleave through impenetrable morass and desert and forest, hostile masses to conquer—a work such as, I am certain, none else had to do before us. (26:464)

I have had my full share of these things and the Mother has had ten times her full share. But that was because the finders of the Way had to face these things in order to conquer. No difficulty that can come on the Sadhak [disciple] but has faced us on the path; against many we have had to struggle hundreds of times (in fact, that is an understatement) before we could overcome; many still remain protesting that they have a right until the perfect perfection is there. But we have never consented to admit their inevitable necessity for others. It is, in fact, to ensure an easier path to others hereafter that we have borne that burden. (26:465)

And he added:

But it is not necessary nor tolerable that all that should be repeated over again to the full in the experience of others. It is because we have the complete experience that we can show a straighter and easier road to others—if they will consent to take it. (26:464)

Mother too, indomitably, descended into the pit:

What I am made to see every night is horrible. Horrible. It's as if one were trying to thoroughly disgust me with my work. That subconscious is truly a mass of horrors. . . . The impression is that it's bottomless and limitless, that there always will be new combinations, always as horrible. But that is not true. It does change. It does change . . . but, oh, what a difficult task! And so intractable. Intractable in that you think you've come to the end of something (you don't think so, you know better than that, but you hope!), and it comes right back in another form, which seems even worse than the previous one! (11/3/62)

I don't know if it's the last battle, but these last few days it has gone down very deep, into the least enlightened part of the cells: what still belongs the most to the world of Unconsciousness and Inertia, what is the most foreign to the divine Presence. You could say it's the original substance used by Life, with a sort of incapacity to respond, to feel any reason for that life. . . . This is an identification with the world at large, with the earth as a whole. An absolutely dreadful and hopeless condition, something that has neither meaning nor goal nor purpose, that lacks any joy of its own and . . . that is worse than unpleasant—meaningless and totally devoid of feeling. Something that has no reason for being, and yet which is. It was . . . it is a dreadful situation.

I have the feeling it's quite close to the bottom. ... And this is the base, the foundation of all materialism. (8/21/63)

The "bottom" has to be cleaned in order for the "top" to accept to come down and materialize in it.

(Sri Aurobindo:) **No, it is not with the Empyrean that I am busy: I wish it were. It is rather with the opposite end of things; it is in the Abyss that I have to plunge to build a bridge between the two. But that too is necessary for my work and one has to face it.** (26:153)

But the joining of the two can also be explosive. For the Light does not tolerate the least speck of dust in its path. Everything it touches must be in the image of its own nature—pure. The least obstacle (or imperfectly purified element) reacts violently, as if violated under the pressure of the unaccustomed Ray. The result in the being, or the beings around—or even in the world around—may take the form of a fine catastrophe.

(Sri Aurobindo:) **The attempt to bring a great general descent having only produced a great ascent of subconscient mud, I had given up that. ... At present I am only trying to prevent people from making hysterical, subconscient asses of themselves, so that I may not be too much disturbed in my operations—not yet with too much success.** (32:389)

(Mother:) It is as though that Force I mentioned were penetrating like a power drill, deeper and deeper toward the subconscious. There are unbelievable things in the subconscious—unbelievable. And it keeps going deeper and deeper ... IMPERATIVELY. So the human subconscious cries out: "Oh, not yet! Please, not yet! Not so fast!" This is what you are up against. It's a general subconscious. (4/12/72)

Perhaps it is what we see everywhere around us?

(Sri Aurobindo:) Things are bad, are growing worse and may at any time grow worst or worse than worst if that is possible—and anything, however paradoxical, seems possible in the present perturbed world. The best thing for them is to realise that all this was necessary because certain possibilities had to emerge and be got rid of, if a new and better world was at all to come into being: it would not have done to postpone them for a later time. It is, as in yoga, where things active or latent in the being have to be put into action in the light so that they may be grappled with and thrown out or to emerge from latency in the depths for the same purificatory purpose. Also they can remember the adage that night is darkest before dawn and that the coming of dawn is inevitable. But they must remember too that the new world whose coming we envisage is not to be made of the same texture as the old and different only in pattern, and that it must come by other means—from within and

not from without; so the best way is not to be too much preoccupied with the lamentable things that are happening outside, but themselves to grow within so that they may be ready for the new world, whatever the form it may take. *[Letter written in July 1948]* (26:1611)

But why, we might ask, is it necessary to confront that horrible subconscious directly? Why can't we keep a "yogic" smile before those base and vulgar things, look at them benignly—from above—and manipulate them with the pincers of a "higher" consciousness and power? Why must we stick our necks out? It is a question that Satprem did not fail to ask Mother:

(Satprem:) **But is it necessary to go down to the level of all these subconscious things? Can one not act on them from above?**

(Mother:) **Act on them from above? . . . I have been acting on them from above for more than thirty years, my child! But it changes nothing— it changes something, but it doesn't transform.**

(Satprem:) **So one must go down to that level?**

(Mother:) **Yes. Acting from above may hold things back, keep them under control, prevent them from taking unpleasant initiatives, but that's not—to transform is to transform.**
As long as we talk of even mastery, it can be done—it can be done very well from above. But, to transform, you must go down, and that's the

terrible part. . . . Otherwise things will never be transformed; they'll remain as they are.
You see, you can even pose as a superman! *(Mother laughs)* But it's still like this *(gesture in midair)*. It isn't the true thing; it isn't the new creation, not the next step of terrestrial evolution. (2/18/61)

Death

Finally, in the subconscious one encounters the ever-present Enemy, the one that has thwarted all our human attempts since the beginning of time, that clips our wings and our dreams in mid-flight despite all our prayers—death. Death, to be sure, does not dream—we will come back to this.

(Sri Aurobindo:) **On life was laid the haunting finger of Death.** (28:208)

Death is the question Nature puts continually to Life and her reminder to it that it has not yet found itself. (16:386)

(Mother:) **Because of physical death, the subconscious is defeatist. You see, whatever progress has been achieved, whatever effort has been exerted, the subconscious has a feeling that things will always end that way, because they have always ended that way until now.** (12/22/71)

Actually, as long as there is death, things will always end badly. (11/13/63)

It's almost as if it were *the* question given me to resolve. (9/28/63)

The Only Solution

The problem is thus set forth: it is global. Nothing can be left out, nothing can remain in the dark, not even a speck of dust. *Everything* must be dealt with, the total world question, otherwise nothing is achieved and nothing is transformed.

Mother and Sri Aurobindo saw the problem very well. They perfectly understood its magnitude and where it plunged its roots. But would they be capable of changing the world alone, of hastening the mutation of the species by going down symbolically into their own body, since everything is one at bottom? What "catastrophes" would they trigger by trying to bring order into an old unrepentant disorder? What subterranean eruptions would the supramental light, which Sri Aurobindo was drawing down day after day into his body, produce? One cannot disturb life's foundations with impunity. Were they not going too fast? Was the world ready for such a drastic change? But, in truth, the world is *never* ready to change! A minimum of willingness is needed on our part, a minimum of blind faith in the future. We have to take the plunge, come what may. The choice is between a long-drawn-out decomposition we know all too well and an unknown future, which can be full of pleasant surprises if we are careful, at each step, to put our endeavor under the protection of the Godhead that guides this universe. At any rate, there seems to be an abundance of signs everywhere: the time for change has come. It is up to each of us to read the signs and quietly set to work, wherever we may be.

Mother and Sri Aurobindo, too, were going to set to work. That "plunge" into the body, into the material consciousness, the consciousness of the cells of the body (the cells have a "consciousness," their own mode of being, otherwise they would not exist), was going to occupy all the time that the disciples were willing to leave them. The disciples were, of course, also part of the "problem"—everything was connected.

> *(Sri Aurobindo:)* **I feel a great longing that the Sadhaks [disciples] should be free of all these strifes and doubts; for so long as the present state of things continues with fires of this kind raging all around and the atmosphere in turmoil, the work I am trying to do (certainly not for my own sake or for any personal reason) will always remain under the stroke of jeopardy and I do not know how the descent I am labouring for is to fulfill itself. In fact, the Mother and I have to give nine-tenths of our energy to smoothing down things, to keeping the Sadhaks tolerably contented etc. etc. etc. One-tenth and in the Mother's case not even that can go to the real work; it is not enough. (26:489)**

Sri Aurobindo, soon followed by Mother, was going to go down into the body. It is hard to imagine what a "sacrifice" this represented for him. All the lights painstakingly conquered "above," all the bliss and "higher powers" are auto-

40

matically annulled, canceled by the still uncultivated ground one goes down into. Everything has to be learned again. There are no more visions, no more spiritual flights, no more interiorization: the laws of matter can only be changed if they are fully assumed.

(Sri Aurobindo:) Working on the physical is like digging the ground; the physical is absolutely inert, dead like stone. When the work began there, all former energies disappeared, experiences stopped; if they came, they didn't last. The process is exceedingly slow. One rises, falls, rises again and falls again, constantly meeting with the suggestions of the Vedic Asuras [devils]: "You can't do anything, you are bound to fail." (34:179)

Mother and Sri Aurobindo had everything to lose by immolating themselves in a substance so contrary to what they were—and they did lose everything . . . to gain everything for the human species.

(Mother:) This is a very humble work in its appearance, very quiet. There are no illuminations filling you with joy. All that is all right for people looking for spiritual joys—that belongs to the past.
. . . All the powers, the siddhis, the realizations, all those things are—they are a big show, a big spiritual show. That's not it! It is very modest— very modest, unassuming, humble, undemonstrative. To get something visible, a tangible

41

result, takes years and years of work, silently, quietly, with great precautions. (8/28/62)

I know perfectly well, because I've had experiences, that when you are satisfied with being a saint or a sage, the whole time you keep the right attitude, everything is fine. The body is not sick, and even if there are attacks, it recovers very easily. Everything is fine ... SO LONG AS THAT WILL FOR TRANSFORMATION DOES NOT EXIST. It's the protest against the will for transformation. Whereas if you say, "All right, fine. Let things be as they are. I don't care, I'm perfectly happy and in a blissful state," the body starts to be happy again! That's it. It's the introduction of something completely new into this matter, and the body protests. (7/15/61)

It isn't a joke, you know, transformation! Yesterday I had such a feeling that ALL the constructions, ALL the habits, the ways of looking at things, the ordinary reactions, all of that was falling to pieces—completely. The impression of being suspended in something . . . completely different, something . . . I don't know. And really the feeling that EVERYTHING one has lived, everything one has known, everything one has done, is a complete illusion. That's what I experienced yesterday evening.

It's one thing to have the spiritual experience that material life is an illusion (some people find it painful, but I found it so extraordinarily beautiful and happy that it was one of the most beau-

tiful experiences of my life), but here it's the
whole spiritual construction as one has lived it
that . . . becomes a complete illusion!—not the
same illusion, but a far more serious illusion.
And I am not exactly a baby—I've been here 47
years! And I have been doing a conscious yoga
for something like . . . yes, certainly 60 years,
with all that memories—the memories of an immortal life—can bring you. And look where I am!
(3/27/61)

It is a slow, meticulous work in which each cell, each atom
must be dealt with and conquered individually.

(Sri Aurobindo:) The physical layer is a very obstinate thing and it requires to be worked out in
detail. You work out one thing and think it is
done; something else arises and you have again
to go over the same ground. It is not like the
mind or the vital where it is easier for the Higher
Power to work. Besides, there—in the mind and
in the vital—you can establish a general law,
leaving out the details; the physical is not so; it
requires constant patience and *minutie* [atten-
tion to details]. (33:309)

(Mother:) From the purely psychological point
of view, it is a relatively easy and swift task, but
when you come to this *(Mother touches her
body)*, to the external form and so-called matter,
oh, it's a world! . . . It's like lessons being given
to you—it's so interesting! Lessons with all the
consequences and explanations. You spend one

day, two days, on a tiny, tiny little discovery.
Then you see, in the body-consciousness, after
that day or those hours of work, that the light is
there, that something is changed—it's changed,
the reactions are no longer the same, but . . .
*(Mother makes a gesture as if to express the
enormous magnitude of the task).* (8/30/67)

There remains to learn how one goes down into a body:
what does it mean practically? What discoveries were Sri
Aurobindo and Mother going to make there? And how can
that mysterious Supermind change our present life in matter and that of the human species in general?

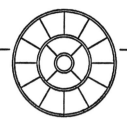

PART TWO

MOTHER

*The Plunge
into the Body*

MOTHER AND SRI AUROBINDO have opened the way to a new species. It is accomplished. For whoever wants to set out, there now exist paths blazed in the horrible subconscious swamp. Matter's terrible inertia has given way; it has been touched and illumined by the higher light. It is the first time that counts. There just remains to follow the signposts and to undergo the experience oneself: to put one's own matter, layer after layer, in contact with "That," as Satprem did after Sri Aurobindo and Mother. It can be done—he has done it. This is not another "spiritual" dream, a nice little meditation on the heights that leaves us physically unchanged; it is a concrete and tangible and transforming reality (and quite formidable, says Satprem). Who wants to try? Do we have that much to lose anyway in leaving the increasingly precarious human groove?

Practically, whoever is interested would simply have to lose himself body and soul in *The Agenda*, the log of Mother's own experience, which she recounted day after day to Satprem during their private conversations. Everything is there for one who knows how to read; the secrets are wide open—it's just a matter of taking the plunge.

The Supramental Force

To give an idea of this *Agenda*, let us listen to Mother describe one of her very first direct experiences with the supramental force, when the connection was made between the heights and the depths. It took place in 1961:

At midnight I was in my bed. And from midnight to 1 o'clock—I was completely awake in my bed; I don't know if my eyes were open or closed, but I was fully awake, NOT IN TRANCE; I could hear every sound, the clocks, etc. Suddenly the whole body (but a slightly larger body, which exceeded the purely physical form) became ONE single vibration, extremely rapid and intense, but immobile. I don't know how you can explain that, because it did not move in space, and yet it was a vibration (that is, it wasn't immobile), but it was immobile in space. It was IN the body, as if there were a vibration in EACH cell and everything were one single vibratory mass. . . . I was absolutely still in my bed. Then, WITHOUT MOVING, without any movement, it began to rise consciously—without moving at all. I was like this *(Mother clasps her hands together and holds them at the level of the forehead as if her whole body were rising like a prayer).* Consciously, like an ascent of this [body-]consciousness toward the supreme Consciousness.
And it kept rising like that, without moving, for a quarter of an hour. The consciousness rose and rose and rose and rose—rose until . . . the junction took place. A completely awake, conscious

junction—NOT IN TRANCE. And the consciousness became the ONE, perfect, eternal consciousness, beyond time, beyond space, beyond
movement, beyond . . . beyond everything—
with, I don't know, an ecstasy, a bliss, something
ineffable.
And it was the consciousness of the BODY.
I had had that experience while being exteri-
orized and in trance, but this time it was THE
BODY, the consciousness of the body. It remained like that for some time (I knew it was a
quarter of an hour because the clock chimed),
but it was absolutely beyond time, you know. It
was an eternity. Then, with the same precision,
the same calm, the same deliberate, clear and
concentrated consciousness (absolutely NOTH-
ING MENTAL), I started to come back down. And
as I was coming down, I noticed that all the difficulties I was struggling with the other day,
which caused that ailment, were ab-so-lute-ly
gone, ANNULLED—mastery. Not even mastery, in
fact: the nonexistence of anything whatsoever
to master; just THE vibration from top to bottom. And there was no more top or bottom or
anything of the sort. (1/24/61)

Such is the first revelation, the first "miracle" of that supramental force: it annuls all our difficulties and human
problems—our "ailments"—as though they DID NOT EXIST
AND HAD NEVER EXISTED. (Yet the illness Mother had been
struggling with for some days was a *physical* illness.) It is
not a "power" that must battle the disorder or illness in order
to impose itself. There is no battle, no effort; it appears and

the illness *no longer exists* (Mother said it was "un-realized," removed from reality).

A phenomenon that gives pause.

Mother would experience that "miracle" hundreds of times, in all sorts of circumstances, for the myriad ills that constantly afflict us: One drop of Supramental on the wound and everything would vanish.

(Mother:) This very morning I was following the movement. I was watching how that vibration of Truth works on certain disorders in the body (tiny bodily problems, you know: discomforts, disorders, and the like). I was watching how that vibration of Truth abolishes those discomforts and disorders. It was very clear, very obvious, and COMPLETELY SEPARATE from any spiritual, religious, or psychological notion, in the sense that, clearly, somebody having that knowledge of opposing one vibration to another wouldn't need to be a "disciple" at all or a man with a philosophical knowledge or anything of the sort; he would just need to master that in order to live a perfectly harmonious existence. It was absolutely concrete and irrefutable. (3/28/64)

The Supramental does not belong to any school. It is not a way of thinking or even praying; it is a *terrestrial*, massive and irrefutable fact.

(Mother:) You know how it is to be really uncomfortable, miserable, to feel nauseous, powerless, to be even incapable of moving, thinking, or anything. Really in a bad way, you know. And all of

a sudden—Consciousness, the bodily consciousness of the vibration of Love, which is the very
essence of creation. Just one second, and everything is illumined—pftt! Gone. Everything is
gone! So you look at yourself in disbelief—it's all
gone. You were feeling really miserable. It's
gone. (11/23/65)

At the beginning Mother was quite surprised. She had
been fighting all her life against the world's darkness in all
its forms. She had given her life to it. It had been a nonstop
battle, day and night, to bring a little harmony and simple
joy to the many wounds of the world, to the men and women
around her as well as to more remote events and difficulties.
But here, suddenly, there was no more struggle. It is as if
the illness or problem vanished into a nonexistence from
which it had perhaps only come out accidentally? In other
words, every time Mother was able to establish the contact
with the Supramental IN HER BODY, the "miracle" happened
again. The world's horror and falsehood disappeared—and
not just in the imagination, but quite concretely and physically (a raging toothache is something quite "concrete"!).
  As the years passed, Mother experienced the phenomenon in herself (when she suffered a physical discomfort or
even a more serious functional disorder, of the heart, for instance), but she also noticed that the same "miracle" could
occur *outside* herself, in the people or circumstances sur-
rounding her, and even at a greater distance on the earth.
She "cured" unwittingly and without moving a finger,
simply by putting the sore point in contact with "that"—and
whether that point was inside her or outside did not seem
to make any difference in the result. The corporeal boundar-
ies had vanished, far and near had vanished, and even time

acted strangely. But let us hear Mother give us a few concrete examples of the behavior of that strange Supramental:

> The experience is repeated in every detail, every kind of situation, like a live demonstration. And it isn't a "long process" of transformation; it's like something suddenly being turned inside out *(Mother twists two of her fingers)*. And instead of seeing ugliness, falsehood, horror, suffering, and all that—suddenly the body lives in bliss. Yet everything is the same; nothing has changed, except consciousness.
>
> The only unknown is how this experience will be translated materially. For this body, it is quite clear: for, say, one or two or three hours, it was in terrible pain; it felt quite miserable (not a moral pain, mind you, a very physical pain), and suddenly, brrff—all gone! ... But that is for one body. What is the effect on others? The body is beginning to perceive the possibility in other consciousnesses as well. From the moral standpoint—that is, attitude, character, reactions—it is quite visible. Sometimes even from the physical standpoint, too: all of a sudden, something disappears—like what we experienced when Sri Aurobindo removed a pain *(Mother makes a gesture showing a hand from the subtle physical taking away the pain)*; we would wonder and ... well, it was gone, vanished! But it isn't yet constant, not established. It's just a proof that it can be like that, since it happens in some instances— it can be like that. (12/21/68)

Time is interminable in the old consciousness, and it no longer exists in this one. I don't know how to describe it. If I used big words, I would say: that old consciousness is ... like death, as though you were going to die at each instant: you're in pain, you—it's the consciousness leading to death. While the other ... *(vast, immutable, smiling gesture)* is life, peaceful life, eternal life. (11/17/71)

There is a strange state of transition in the most material consciousness, the consciousness of the body. A transition from that state of subjugation, powerlessness, in which you are constantly at the mercy of forces, vibrations, unexpected movements, all sorts of stray impulses—and Power. Power asserting itself and realizing itself. It's a transition between the two, with all sorts of experiences, from the most mental part of that consciousness to the most obscure, the most material. It's a transition between almost total powerlessness—a kind of Fate, the imposition of a whole set of determinisms against which you can do nothing, which crush you— and a clear, defined Will, which is all-powerful as soon as *it* expresses itself. (1/15/64)

It's—yes, I think the only word to describe the sensation one has is *absolute*—an absolute. That's the sensation: to experience the Absolute. The Absolute—absolute Knowledge, absolute Will, absolute Power. Nothing, absolutely nothing can resist. And it's an absolute that is so merciful! It's something next to which everything we consider kind and merciful is—oof, nothing whatsoever! It is Mercy together with absolute power. It is not Wisdom, not Knowledge, it's—it has nothing to do with our ways. For several hours, never has this body, in the ninety-one years it has been on this earth, felt such a happiness: freedom, absolute power, and no limits *(gesture here and there and everywhere)*, no limits, no impossibility, nothing. (2/15/69)

And absolutely everything, every circumstance, is as catastrophic as can be: problems, complications, difficulties, everything is raging furiously like wild animals—but it's over. The body KNOWS it's over. It may take centuries, but it's over. It may take centuries to disappear, but it is now over. It is now sure, absolutely sure and certain *(Mother lowers a finger)*, that the very concrete and absolute realization one could only have when one left matter will be possible RIGHT HERE. (3/14/70)

The Work

Mother's only work (if one may say so!) was to put more and more material substance in contact with that supramental light.

(Mother:) The education of the physical consciousness (not the body's global consciousness, but the consciousness of the cells) consists in

teaching them, first, that there is a choice (it appears as a choice): to choose the divine Presence, the divine Consciousness, the divine Power (all this without words), the "something" that we define as the absolute Master. It is a choice of *every second* between Nature's old laws, together with some mental influence and the whole life such as it is organized—a choice between that, the rule of that, and the rule of the supreme Consciousness. And it's every second of the day (it's infinitely interesting), with practical examples —for instance, the nerves: If a nerve obeys this or that law of Nature, together with the mental conclusions and all that—all that machinery— then the pain starts up; but if it obeys the influence of the supreme Consciousness, then a curious thing happens: it isn't like something getting "cured"; rather, it's as if it disappeared as a sort of unreality. (6/26/68)

The cells must learn to seek their support *only* in the Divine, until such time as they can feel they are the expression of the Divine.... This is what I am experiencing now. I do have the experience of changing the effect of things, but it isn't mentalized, so I can't express it in words. But, truly, what is important is that the cells should feel, first, that they are entirely governed by the Divine (which is translated by the state of "what You will, what You will . . . "), then a sort of receptivity (what shall I say? . . .), not immobile, but . . . one could probably call it a *passive* receptivity. *(Mother opens her hands in a smile)* I don't know how to explain. All words are wrong, but one could say: "You alone exist." The cells should feel: "You alone exist." Like that. But all this seems so hard—the words harden the experience. It's a sort of plasticity or suppleness (a trusting, very trusting suppleness): what You will, what You will. . . . (10/16/71)

The work, you see, consists in changing the conscious base of all the cells—but not all at once! That would be impossible. Even little by little, it's very difficult. The moment the conscious base changes, it's—there's almost like a panic in the cells and the feeling: "Oh, what's going to happen to me?" So from time to time, it's difficult. They are taken in groups, almost by faculty or part of faculty, and for some it's a little difficult. Sometimes there is almost an anguish, you know. You're suspended in nothing. It may last a few seconds, but those few seconds are terrible. (2/19/69)

The Unreality

She kept cleaning and cleaning the "intermediate layers" that prevent total contact, all the sediment that human habit has deposited in our bodies and that seems to encase us in a deadly matrix in which *everything* is catastrophic, *everything* can become an accident or an illness, *everything* can go wrong—truly as if we were enclosed, locked up in an unreal world and we had only to remove that matrix, to let

a little light penetrate into the cells, for *everything* to change
(that is, for us to leave the unreality of a world we call real).

(Mother:) **It's like something sticky all around
you, touching you everywhere. You cannot take
one step, cannot do anything without encoun-
tering the black and sticky fingers of Falsehood.**
(12/31/63)

**And what is this creation? Well, separation and
malice, cruelty (a thirst to hurt, one could say),
and suffering (the joy of making others suffer),
disease and decomposition and death—destruc-
tion. All this is part of the same thing. What has
happened?! ... And the experience I had was the
UNREALITY of those things, as if we had entered
an unreal falsehood and everything disappears
when we get out of it—it no longer exists, no
longer is. This is what is so frightening! That it
should be, for us, so real, so concrete, so dreadful—and none of it exists. It's only—we've
entered Falsehood. Why? How? What? (5/31/69)**

**Why, all sensations are false, my child! It's some-
thing I've experienced dozens of times a day, in
every detail. You feel you need this, need that,
you hurt here, hurt there—but it's all false. In
fact, you have left the state of Harmony, that
Harmony which is always present—but you've
left it, and you need this, need that, hurt here,
hurt there. Something is missing, and That is
what is missing. (7/10/65)**

This is really something! Why didn't we think of it before! All our ills are false, our pain is false, our ignorance and weaknesses are false, and even our "laws" are false. We are merely shut inside a "room" of *unreality*, which exists solely by the recognition we lend to it. We just have to get out—or stop believing in it—and that'll be it. However, one does not get out in one's head, or through transcendental meditation; one gets out in one's cells. Unless we go down to *that* level, we will keep building castles in the air.

(Mother:) **From the negative standpoint—I am talking of the difficulties to be overcome—one of the most serious obstacles is the legitimacy that the ignorant and false external consciousness, the ordinary consciousness, gives to all the so-called physical laws, causes, effects and consequences—to all that science has discovered in the material and physical realm. All that is indisputable reality for the consciousness, a reality that stands independent and absolute in the face of the eternal divine Reality. And it is so automatic that it's unconscious. (5/10/58)**

The moment the body becomes conscious, it becomes conscious of its own falsehood! It becomes conscious of this law, that law, that third law, that fourth law, that tenth law—everything is "laws." "We are ruled by the physical law: such a thing will produce such a result, and if you do this, such and such will happen, etc." Why, it oozes from every pore! I know it. I know it very well. It exudes falsehood. In the body, we have no faith in the divine Grace—none, none, none

whatsoever! If we have not undergone tapasya [yogic discipline] the way I have, we say, "Well, all the inner, moral things, all the feelings and psychology are all very well; we want the Divine and we are ready to do anything; but, nonetheless, material facts are material facts; they are concrete and real: an illness is an illness, food is food, and the consequence of all we do is a consequence, and if—blah, blah, blah, blah, blah, blah!"
We have to understand that this isn't true—it isn't true. It's a lie. It's nothing but a big lie. It isn't true—it is NOT true! (5/10/58)

All the constraints, all the attachments to external things, all that is finished, completely over with, completely over—absolute freedom. I mean, there's only That left, the Supreme Master, who is master. From that standpoint, it can only be a gain. It is such a radical realization. . . . It seems like an absolute of freedom, something considered impossible to realize while living a normal life on earth. It's equivalent to the experience of absolute freedom one has in the higher parts of the being when the dependence on the body has been removed. But what's remarkable (I want to emphasize this) is that it's the consciousness of *the body* that experiences all this—and a body that is visibly still here! (3/9/66)

Back and Forth

So she went constantly from one world to another, from this one, so compellingly real and true for us, to the other, no less real, but of a . . . smiling reality.

(Mother:) **It's quite extraordinary. There is something happening to me all the time, at least fifty times a day (it's especially clear at night): outwardly, it's as if you moved from one room to another, or from one house to another, but you cross the threshold, or go through the wall, without being aware of it, automatically. Being in one room is translated outwardly by a very comfortable condition, completely free of any pain anywhere, and by a great peace—a joyous, perfectly quiet peace—in a word, an ideal state that lasts sometimes a long, long time. . . . Then, all of a sudden, for no perceptible or apparent reason (I still haven't been able to figure out why or how), you—it's as if you fell into the other room, or other house, as if you tripped; and you start feeling a pain here, a pain there; you're uncomfortable. (5/31/62)**

There's a curious sensation, a peculiar perception of the two functionings—which are not even . . . you can't even say they are "superimposed"— the true functioning and the functioning distorted by the individual sense of an individual body. They are almost simultaneous, which is what makes it so difficult to explain. . . . There are a lot of things not functioning properly in

the body (I don't know if you would call them illnesses—maybe doctors would, I don't know, but
at any rate, it's something not functioning properly), organs not functioning properly: heart,
stomach, intestines, lungs, etc.; and at the same
time (you can't really call it a "functioning"), the
true state. Which means that certain disorders
appear only when the consciousness is—it's as
though the consciousness were pulled or push-
ed, or placed, in a certain position, and then
those improper functionings appear *instantly*,
but not as a consequence (I mean, the consciousness just becomes aware of their existence). And
if the consciousness remains long enough in that
position, there are what we usually call consequences: the improper functioning has consequences. . . . But if the consciousness regains
its true position, it stops instantly. And sometimes it's like this *(Mother places the fingers of
her open right hand between those of her open
left hand to show overlapping or interpenetra-
tion)*, I mean, like this and that, like this and that
*(Mother moves the fingers of her right hand back
and forth between those of her left hand to show
a sort of coming and going of consciousness between two states)*, this position and that position,
this one and that one. It goes from one to the
other in a matter of a few seconds, so you can almost perceive the two functionings simultaneously. That's how I was able to understand what
was happening to me, otherwise I wouldn't have
understood. I would only have thought I was in
a particular state, then slipped into another

state. It isn't so; it's—everything, all the substance, all the vibrations must follow their normal course, you see—it's just the perception of the consciousness that is altered.

Which means that if we push this knowledge to its limit, that is, if we generalize, life (what we generally call "life," physical life, the life of the body) and death ARE ONE AND THE SAME THING. They are simultaneous. . . . It's only consciousness doing this and doing that, moving this way or that way *(same coming and going gesture of the fingers)*. I don't know if I am making sense, but it's fantastic. (9/8/62)

What is becoming very clear is that, although everything remains the same and the position of the consciousness remains the same, there occurs a reversal from this way to that way *(Mother turns her hand from one side to the other)*. I don't know how to explain. In one case, I mean for the ordinary human consciousness (not ordinary, but present), the pain is almost unbearable; and while everything remains *exactly the same*, with that little reversal (I don't know how to describe it, perhaps you could call it "contact with the Divine," I don't know), while everything remains the same (it's a phenomenon of consciousness)—a marvelous bliss, with every physical circumstance IDENTICAL, you understand. . . . And I experience this all the time. Unfortunately *(Mother laughs)*, the painful side is the longer of the two! When I am quiet, still, then naturally the other takes over.

Even a toothache and all that, which, externally, for the material consciousness, is so real(!)— even that is no longer ... When the true consciousness takes over it no longer has the same character. I don't know how to explain it. There must be what we would call a "cure" in our ordinary consciousness, but it isn't a cure; the nature of it changes. (7/11/70)

What Sri Aurobindo says here about illnesses is exactly what I am experiencing: the force of habit and all the mental constructions, all that seems "inevitable" and "irrevocable" in illnesses. It's as if examples were multiplying in order to demonstrate ... so we can learn that it's only a question of attitude—of attitude—a question of going beyond . . . beyond that mental prison in which humanity has locked itself up, and . . . of breathing above.
And that's what *the body* is experiencing. Before, those who had inner experiences would say, "True, it's that way up above, but here ... " Now the "but here" will soon no longer apply. That's the conquest we are in the process of making, the momentous change: that physical life should be ruled by the higher consciousness and not by the mental world. It's the "change of government." . . . It's difficult, laborious, painful; there's some breakage, naturally, but . . . But, truly, there's a change—a visible change. And that's the true change; it's what will enable the new Consciousness to express itself. The body is

learning. It is learning its lesson—all bodies, all
bodies. (3/14/70)

A Body Still Human

And how does a poor little human body, made of a still
ordinary substance, withstand all those transits, that movement back and forth between one world and another? It
must not know where it stands anymore!

(Mother:) **Every time the rule or domination of
Nature's ordinary laws is replaced at one point
or another (or must be replaced or is about to be
replaced at any point) by the authority of the
divine Consciousness, that creates a state of
transition that has every appearance of a frightful disorder and a very great danger. And so long
as the body does not know, as long as it is in its
state of ignorance, it is thrown into a panic and
thinks it's a serious illness—and sometimes,
with the help of the imagination, it does become
a serious illness. Yet, originally, it isn't that; it's
just the withdrawal of the rule of ordinary Nature, with its auxiliary of personal vital and
mental laws. (2/3/68)**

**It is very difficult for the body to change, be-
cause it lives only out of habit. So every time
something of the new way of living slips in, free
of thought, free of reasoning, free of anything re-
sembling an idea, almost free of sensation—almost automatically—the newness of it throws**

the cells into a panic. So EVERYTHING has to be changed, you see. It's no longer the heart that must pump the blood or receive the Force; it's no longer the stomach that must digest the food, no longer all that—it must function in another way. The base of it all must be changed, the functioning completely modified—while every single one of these cells tries to make sure that everything should work as usual!

Terrible. A strange difficulty.

If the inner being—the true being—is in control, the body does things automatically, through the power of the true being; but then, it doesn't become conscious of its own change; it doesn't collaborate in the change; and it might take . . . maybe thousands of years for the change to occur. The true being must remain like this *(gesture of stepping back, of remaining in the background)*, and the body must do things by itself. That is, it must hold the Lord, receive the Lord, offer itself to the Lord, BE the Lord. It does have the aspiration, oh, quite intense—it's blazing— that part is all right. But the Lord *(smiling)* doesn't work in the usual way! And the moment He simply tries to take control of one function or another, even partially (not totally), all the relations, all the movements are instantly altered—panic. Panic at that particular point. The result: you faint, or you are on the verge of fainting, or you are seized with horrible pain, or at any rate something apparently becomes extremely upset. So what is to be done? . . . Wait patiently until that small number or large num-

ber of cells, that little corner of consciousness, has learned its lesson. It takes one day, two days, three days, and that "great" traumatic event quiets down, becomes clarified, and those particular cells say to themselves (they begin to), "God, how stupid we are! . . . " It takes a little while. Now they've understood.
But there are thousands upon thousands upon thousands of them! (1/9/63)

All of a sudden the body finds itself . . . outside of all habits, all actions, reactions, consequences, etc., and that's . . . *(Mother opens her eyes in wonder)*, then it goes away. It's so new for the material consciousness that, every time, you feel on the verge of mental derangement (or rather, derangement of *consciousness*, not mental derangement; happily, it has nothing to do with the mind!). But for a minute the consciousness panics. . . . The body has enough sense to—it *knows* it isn't ill—it knows it isn't an illness; it's just an attempt at transformation. It knows it full well, but . . . there are all those centuries of habit. (5/20/70)

"The Divine"

Mother was really the focal point of an impossible contradiction. Through a body constituted and formed in the ordinary way, she was in touch with a world totally contrary to the ordinary way, a world where our good and evil no longer had the same meaning, where the fixity of our laws, the

sense of finiteness, distance, and even time, became something different, . . . which Mother liked to call "the Lord,"
that is, a "something" one still cannot name without using
circumlocutions, yet which seemed endowed with a very concrete reality since "He" directed everything in the body at
every second of life.

> *(Mother:)* I say "the Divine"—what is the
> "Divine"? Well, I don't know—and I can't say
> that I don't know, either. And even saying that
> is wrong. That's not it. Everything is NOT IT.
> (10/13/71)

> But the body has learned that, even without ego,
> it is what it is; for it is that by the divine Will and
> not at all by the ego—we exist by the divine Will
> and not by the ego. The ego has been a means—
> a centuries-old means. Now it is worthless; its
> time is over. It has had its time, its usefulness—
> it's over, it's the past, far back in the past. Now
> ... *(Mother lowers her fist)* it's consciousness, it's
> the Divine—individuality is the Divine.

> And this body has clearly understood, felt, "re-
> alized," as they say in English, that the sense of
> being a separate personality is totally unneces-
> sary, TOTALLY unnecessary, not in the least in-
> dispensable to its existence. It exists by another
> power and another will, which is not individual
> or personal—the divine Will. And it will become
> what it is supposed to be only when it feels
> there's no difference between it and the Divine.
> That's all. Everything else is falsehood—false,

67

false, false—and a falsehood that must go.
There's only *one* reality, only *one* life, only *one*
consciousness *(Mother lowers her fist)*—the
Divine. (6/9/71)

There was such a sense of warmth, of intimacy,
of . . . sweetness, and such a power at the same
time, oh, so concrete! The whole atmosphere, the
whole atmosphere had become concrete: everything, but everything tasted like the Lord. I
don't know how to explain that. It was completely material, as if I had a mouthful of it! It
was everywhere, in everything. And so PHYSI-
CAL! Like—you could compare it to the most
delicious taste you can experience (it had a very,
very material feel and taste to it). It's as if you
could feel something solid in your hand when
you closed it—such a warm and sweet and
powerful vibration, so powerful, so concrete!
(5/19/61)

The Transformation of the Body

Nonetheless, there still remained the fundamental question of a body made in an old, outmoded way, which had to
respond and function in the new way. . . .

(Sri Aurobindo:) It might be that a psychological
change, a mastery of the nature by the soul, a
transformation of the mind into a principle of
light, of the life-force into power and purity
would be the first approach, the first attempt to

68

solve the problem, to escape beyond the merely human formula and establish something that could be called a divine life upon earth, a first sketch of supermanhood, of a supramental being living in the circumstances of the earth-nature. But this could not be the complete and radical change needed; it would not be the total transformation, the fullness of a divine life in a divine body. There would be a body still human and indeed animal in its origin and fundamental character and this would impose its own inevitable limitations on the higher parts of the embodied being. As limitation by ignorance and error is the fundamental defect of an untransformed mind, as limitation by the imperfect impulses and strainings and wants of desire are the defects of an untransformed life-force, so also imperfection of the potentialities of the physical action, an imperfection, a limitation in the response of its half-consciousness to the demands made upon it and the grossness and stains of its original animality would be the defect of an untransformed or imperfectly transformed body. These could not but hamper and even pull down towards themselves the action of the higher parts of the Nature. A transformation of the body must be the condition for a total transformation of the nature. (16:21)

(Mother:) Take the change in the functioning of the organs, for example. What is the procedure? And both [ways] are already starting to exist side by side. . . . What is required for one to dis-

appear and for the other to stay all by itself, changed? Changed, because as it is now, it would not be sufficient to make the body function; there are all those functions the body must still perform which it couldn't perform. It would stay in a blissful state, would enjoy its condition—but it couldn't enjoy it for long, for all its needs would still be there! This is the difficulty. Those who come later, in a hundred years, two hundred years, won't have these difficulties. They will just have to choose: no longer to belong to the old system or to belong to the new. But at present? . . . A stomach must digest, you see! There has to be a new way of adapting oneself to the forces of Nature, a new functioning. (2/13/62)

When you think about it, it's easy enough to understand: if the question were merely to stop something and begin something ELSE, it could be done rather swiftly. But to keep a body alive (to keep it working, that is) while, *at the same time*, introducing a new functioning adequate enough to keep the body alive, and a transformation—that makes for a kind of very difficult combination to realize. . . . Especially, you see, as regards the heart. The heart replaced by the center of Power, a formidable dynamic power! *(Mother laughs)* At what *moment* do you suppress the circulation and throw in the Force?? (10/6/62)

70

It's a hundred times more wonderful than we
can ever imagine. The problem is to know whether this *(pointing to the body)* will be able to follow.... To follow means not only to last, but to
acquire new strength and a new life. That I don't
know. (10/30/71)

The contradiction, the tension in that body was tremendous. Things could not last that way—something had
to give or ... Or what?

(Mother:) It [the body] says, "Actually, it's especially for others that it would make a difference
[if it died]! For me, it's ... " Because, you see,
they are still in that sort of illusion that one dies
when the body dies. But even this [Mother's
body] is not sure which is true anymore!... For
the body, it should be matter that is the truth—
but then, even it is not too sure *(laughing)* what
matter is anymore! There is the other, the other
way of looking at things and feeling and being—
another way of being. So the body is beginning
to wonder.... It knows the old way is finished,
but it's beginning to wonder what it will be like,
that is, the way of perceiving, of relating to
things: "What sort of relation will the new consciousness have with the old consciousness of
those who are still human? ... " All things will
remain as they are, but there will be a new way
of perceiving them, a new relationship. ... It
comes—it's strange, it comes like a breath and
then goes away again. Like a breath of a new
way of looking at things, a new way of feeling, of

71

hearing. It's like something getting closer and then being veiled. And then, the appearance [of Mother's body] is . . . *(Mother makes a chaotic gesture)*. Yet, quite visibly, I am not sick, but there are moments when . . . it's very difficult. Very difficult. And several times, I have experienced both [ways] at the same time. . . . So *(laughing)* the body says to itself, "Well, if they only knew what you're going through, they'd say you are mad as a hatter!" (4/29/70)

You know, that whole base—from automatism to all the movements we make out of habit (there's an enormous quantity of things we do automatically)—is gone. And so it's . . . difficult. . . . Especially—especially eating, because for a very long time now (many, many years), I've had no interest in food, none whatever. I take it only . . . I take it with a certain knowledge of what's necessary, and that's it. But now it's . . . almost difficult to swallow. That's the main problem: a great difficulty swallowing. . . . I have some trouble breathing, too. I am short-winded. What is going to happen? I have no idea. *(Mother laughs)* (4/8/70)

As it undergoes its transfer of authority (what I call the transfer of authority), the body goes through difficult moments, truly difficult moments. And by normal standards it doesn't make any sense because the difficulties seem to increase with what could be called the "conversion"—but . . . for the true vision (when you are

in the true vision), it's the rest of the **Falsehood**
that causes all the problems. (1/31/70)

The Walk in the Dark

Mother was full of questions. The future seemed so mysterious. She had to take each step in the dark, in total un-
knowingness. (If one knew beforehand the fate of the new
species, it would be there already.)

(Mother:) These last few days, I have been looking. . . . This path has never been followed by
anyone! Sri Aurobindo was the first one and he
left before telling us what he was doing. I am absolutely blazing a trail in a jungle—worse than
a jungle. For the last two days, the feeling of
knowing *absolutely* nothing—nothing. (7/15/61)

The first time I saw Sri Aurobindo, he told me,
"Others came to prepare the way and they left,
but this time, it's to DO." And he, too, left.
He left. He did tell me, "*You* will do it." But he
said it "like that," the way he used to say things,
you know. It was not a statement that gives you
an absolute certitude. . . .
I can't say that I am raising the question, because I am not—I am not raising it—but both
possibilities are there *(suspended gesture)*, and
neither gets answered. There are times when I
have the vision that the end is near (a very practical vision of the things I need to do)—it comes,
but against a backdrop of complete uncertainty.

**And the next minute comes the possibility to go
through to the end of the transformation, with
a clear vision of what needs to be done, but the
background is . . . there's no Assurance in the
background that it WILL BE SO. Neither in one
case nor in the other. And I know it's deliberate,
because it's necessary for the work in the cells.
If, for example, I received the Command of the
Supreme (I do receive it sometimes, clear, as
clear as . . .), if I received from Him the certitude
that, whatever the appearances of the path, this
body will go through to the end of the transformation, well, there would be some slackening
somewhere, and that would be very detrimental.
(9/25/65)**

The only solution was to go on, to continue to incarnate
that new way of being on earth in the minutest details of
life. And perhaps the Supramental had more than one surprise up its sleeve? What seems impossible and contradictory today might not be so tomorrow? All the same, that
transition from one way to another, from one body to another
preoccupied Mother very much. . . .

**Sometimes, I wonder if it isn't sheer madness to
want to attempt this. . . . Shouldn't I simply let
this body dissolve and let other, better-adapted
bodies be prepared? I don't know. I don't know,
you see! No one has done it before, so there's
nobody to tell me. (2/13/62)**

**When you have someone who has gone through
the experience and has naturally Wisdom, it's so**

74

simple! Before, for the least thing, I didn't even have to say anything to Sri Aurobindo and it was taken care of. Now, it's I who am doing the work, and I have nobody to turn to; nobody has done it! So that, too, is a source of tension. (8/26/64)

I hope this body is capable. There's that doubt, you see.

(Satprem:) Of course you're capable, Mother. This is the time to do it, otherwise you wouldn't be here. If you are here, in this condition, it's precisely because the time has come.

(Mother:) Yes, naturally! I know—of course, I know this is the time when . . . This is the time to make the Attempt, but is it going to succeed? I don't know. . . . Is it—to put things more clearly, if you will—is it *destined* to succeed? There lies the doubt. Is it destined to succeed?

(Satprem:) To me, it just seems impossible not to—it's impossible for it not to succeed.

(Mother:) Why?

(Satprem:) Because you're the body of the world! Because this is really the Hope.

(Mother:) Isn't that poetry?

(Satprem:) Of course not, Mother! That's really how it is. One just has to look around: the world is more and more hellish.

(Mother:) Oh, yes. Quite true.

(Satprem:) Well, that's what is in your body. (9/12/70)

I have the feeling that if I last till I am a hundred (which means another six years), much will be

accomplished—much. **Something important
and decisive will be accomplished.** I am not saying that the body will be capable of transforming itself (I have no indication of that), but the
consciousness—the physical, material consciousness becoming . . . "supramentalized."
That's it; that's the work being done now. And
that's what's important. (4/26/72)

The Contagion

On the positive side, if we may say so, there were two fac-
tors that, sooner or later, seemed to guarantee the success
of the undertaking.

The first was that new way of being on earth was clearly
contagious from one body to another. Fortunately, our bodies are not shut in separate little boxes the way our heads
are! Made from the same mold, our cells have their own
means of communication, and whatever is acquired by one
is sooner or later passed on to another. Thus, there was "contagion" around Mother.

(Satprem:) **I well understand that certain things
are happening in you, but . . .**
(Mother:) **Look, if they are happening in one
body, they can happen in all bodies! I am not
made of anything different from others. The
difference is consciousness. That's all. This body
is made exactly in the same way, with the same
things. I eat the same things, and it was formed
in the same way, absolutely. And it was as
stupid, as obscure, as unconscious, as stubborn**

76

as all the other bodies in the world.

It all began when the doctors declared that I was very ill—that was the beginning [in April 1962]. Because the body was then completely drained of its habits and strength, which allowed the cells slowly, very slowly to awaken to a new receptivity and open themselves directly to the divine Influence. Each cell is vibrating.

Otherwise, it would be hopeless! If this substance, which began as—even a stone has already some form of organization—it was certainly worse than a stone: absolute, inert unconsciousness. Then it slowly, very slowly, awakens.... For the animal to become a man, it took nothing but the infusion of a consciousness —a mental consciousness—and what's happening now is the awakening of the consciousness that was in the depths, all the way down in the depths. The mind was withdrawn, the vital was withdrawn, everything was withdrawn—when I was supposedly ill, the mind was gone, the vital was gone, and the body was left on its own—on purpose. And it's just because the mind and vital were gone that there was that impression of a serious illness. But in the body left on its own, the cells slowly began to awaken to consciousness *(ascending gesture of aspiration)*. After both the mind and vital were gone, the consciousness that had been infused into the body BY the vital (from the mind into the vital and from the vital into the body) slowly began to emerge. It began with that explosion of Love all the way up above, at the extreme supreme altitude, and it slowly, very slowly came down into the body. And that sort of physical mind—something really quite stupid that used to go round and round, forever repeating the same thing, the same thing a hundred times—gradually became enlightened, conscious, organized, and fell silent. And from that silence rose an aspiration expressed by prayers.

This is the complete denial of all past spiritual assertions: "If you want to live a fully conscious divine life, you must leave your body; the body cannot follow." Well, Sri Aurobindo came and said, "Not only can the body follow, but it can be the basis for manifesting the Divine."

The work remains to be done. . . .

But it's all ONE SINGLE substance, exactly the same everywhere, which was unconscious everywhere. And what's remarkable is that, automatically, some very unexpected experiences are happening here and there *(gesture indicating scattered points throughout the world)*, in people who don't even know anything. (11/22/67)

I'll soon become dangerously contagious, you know! (4/4/70)

But once it is done—that's what Sri Aurobindo had said—once *one* body has done it, it becomes capable of passing it on to others. And, as I mentioned, there is now (I am not speaking of a total and detailed phenomenon, certainly not), but there is here and there *(gesture showing scattered points on the earth)* one experience or another suddenly happening in people. It's contagious. I know it! And that's the only hope, because if everybody had to go through the same experience.... (11/22/67)

No More Wear and Tear

The second factor comes to light through experience: When the body was in the harmonious position, the erosion of time no longer existed. There was no more friction with life's circumstances, no "jagged edges" anywhere; everything became a vast and harmonious—"divine"—unfolding, like great undulating waves, from morning breakfast to the swarm of disciples who still had to be seen every day. The body thus seemed to be able to last an eternity.

(Mother:) **The conditions for prolonging the body almost indefinitely are known or almost known (they are more than just an inkling; they are known). And they are learned through the work necessary to counteract the EXTREME FRAGILITY of the physical balance of the body in transformation. It's a study of each minute, as it were, almost of each second. (4/17/65)**

You see, my body is beginning—beginning—to understand that the divine side means a life that is ... *(Mother opens her arms in an immense gesture)* **progressive and luminous. But there's the accumulation of past experiences that says, "Oh, this isn't possible!" That's it. And that stupid "not possible" is what delays and spoils things.**

It's based on the fact that the minute the body leaves the true attitude it becomes painful: everything starts to hurt, to be laborious—you have the feeling of death and dissolution in everything. And this is what strengthens . . . matter's stupidity. (8/30/72)

Sri Aurobindo had said, "The intermediate stage will be prolongation of life at will." And my impression is that it's possible. But on the condition that . . . the body itself have only one idea: transformation. It has to be quiet, concentrated . . . I can stay for hours like that, in a sort of receptive contemplation, and it seems like a second. Time, yes, is curious. There is a certain receptive contemplation in which . . . *(suspended gesture with a smile)* time ceases to exist. (9/4/71)

But every time I ask my body what *it* would like, all the cells say, "No, no! We are immortal; we want to be immortal. We are not tired; we are ready to fight for centuries if necessary. We have been created for immortality and we want immortality." I am realizing that the nearer you get to the cell, the more the cell says, "But I am immortal!" (10/16/62)

Everything Is Going There

Thus, one could hope that the contagion would spread, first in the human bodies around Mother, then perhaps at greater distances around the earth. And since the body could in principle last indefinitely, one could look forward to a constant progression, a "densification" of the new Possibility, which would gradually, at its own rhythm, carry out the necessary bodily mutations and change our human world into an entirely supramental world in a continuous and harmonious fashion.

But this is perhaps too human and "logical" a way to envision the transformation of the world into a world of harmony. The Supramental has its own laws, which are infinitely flexible and wise. The Supramental is also infinite compassion; it takes the present conditions of the earth into account in all its operations. It does not destroy, does not break; it simply puts things before their content of truth... until they have had enough of their current falsehood. It is not in a hurry, for it is supreme. It is *at the heart* of all things, their springs and intimate hope. If evolution cannot follow this path, well, it will follow another! We are all going there anyway, for *everything* is going there.

(Sri Aurobindo:) **The obscurations of earth will not prevail against the supramental truth-consciousness, for even into the earth it can bring enough of the omniscient light and omnipotent force of the spirit to conquer. All may not open to the fullness of its light and power, but whatever does open must to that extent undergo the change. That will be the principle of transformation.** (1:20)

What the supramental will do the mind cannot foresee or lay down. The mind is ignorance seeking for the Truth, the supramental by its very

definition is the Truth-Consciousness, Truth in possession of itself and fulfilling itself by its own power. In a supramental world imperfection and disharmony are bound to disappear.... But what, how, by what degrees it will do it, is a thing that ought not to be said now—when the Light is there, the Light will itself do its work—when the supramental Will stands on earth, that Will will decide. It will establish a perfection, a harmony, a Truth-creation—for the rest, well, it will be the rest—that is all. (22:12)

(Mother:) I have here all the examples, a small sampling of all the attitudes, and I clearly see the reactions; I see the same Force, the same unique Force, acting in that sampling and producing naturally different results, but for a more profound vision those "differences" are very superficial: it's only "they like to think that way, so let them think that way." But the actual inner progress, the inner development, the essential vibration, is not affected—not in the least. One person aspires with all his heart for Nirvana, another aspires with all his might for the supramental manifestation, and in both the vibratory result is about the same. It's all one single mass of vibrations getting more and more prepared to ... receive what has to be. (5/19/65)

We consider this appearance *(Mother points to her body)* as ... for the ordinary consciousness, it seems to be the most important—it's obviously the last thing that will change. For the ordinary consciousness, it's the last thing that will change because it's the most important: that will be the surest sign. But it isn't that way at all! Not at all. It's the change IN THE CONSCIOUSNESS—which has taken place—that is the important thing. All the rest is consequences. But here, in this world, this material world, it seems the most important because it's—it's completely upside down. For us, when the body can be visibly other than it is now, we will say, "Ah, now the thing is done." Not so—the thing IS done. This [the body] is a secondary consequence. (4/29/70)

The Battle of the World

In any case, very practically, Mother's body was the site of a gigantic battle extending far beyond the limits of a small human body. In her body was being played out something like the future of the world.

(Mother:) It's really interesting. It's as though my body were the site of a battle between what wants obstinately to hang on and what wants to take its place. There are truly marvelous moments—glorious moments—and the next second or next minute such a violent attack! That's the situation. And my body is . . . For food, for example, there are times when I eat without even noticing I am eating, except that everything tastes delicious; and the next second, I can't swallow a thing! It's like this *(gesture of being pulled from one side to the other)*. So my only so-

lution is to be as quiet as possible. As soon as I am quiet, it calms down. Suddenly, you get the feeling you're about to die, and the next minute it's ... eternity. It's truly an extraordinary experience. Extraordinary. There comes a moment when everything, absolutely everything seems to be full of confusion and darkness—there's no hope, no chance of seeing things clearly—and the next minute, everything is crystal clear. (11/13/71)

You see, the little body ... the little body is like a point, but it feels like the expression of a *tremendous* power, and yet it is rather ... : no capacity, no expression, nothing—and rather ... miserable. And yet ... it is like a condensation —the condensation of a TREMENDOUS power! Sometimes it's even difficult to bear. (9/2/70)

I am absolutely convinced (because I have had experiences to prove it) that the life of this body —what makes it move, evolve—can be replaced by a force. I mean, it's possible to achieve a sort of immortality, and the wear and tear can also disappear. These are the two things possible: the force of life can come and the wear and tear can disappear. And it can come psychologically, through complete obedience to the divine Impulsion, which means that at each instant you have the force that is necessary, you do the thing that is necessary—all these are certitudes. Absolute certitudes. It is not hope, not imagination; it's a certitude. It's just a question of education and slow transformation, of changing the habits. It's possible—all this is possible. The only thing is, how long will it take to eliminate the necessity of a skeleton (to take only this example)? That seems to me to be still very far ahead. I mean, it will still require many intermediate stages. Sri Aurobindo said that one can prolong life indefinitely. That part is clear. But we are not yet built with a substance that completely escapes dissolution, the necessity of dissolution. The bones last a long time; in favorable conditions, they can even last a thousand years, but that doesn't mean immortality *in principle*. ... I can conceive of a perpetual change; I could even conceive of a flower that would not wither. But this principle of immortality ... That is, a life basically escaping the necessity for renewal, a life in which the eternal Force manifests itself directly and eternally, and yet in a body that is physical *(Mother touches the skin of her hands)*. I can readily accept a progressive change that would make this substance into something capable of eternally renewing itself from inside out—and that would be immortality—but it seems to me that many steps would be necessary between what exists now, what we are at present, and that other life mode. For instance, if you asked these cells, with all the consciousness and experience they now have, "Is there anything you are incapable of doing?," in all sincerity they will reply, "No! Whatever the Lord wants, I can do." That's their state of consciousness. But in the appearance, it's different. My personal experience is this: all I do with the Presence of the Lord, I do without effort, without difficulty, without fatigue or wear and tear, like this *(Mother extends both arms in a great harmonious Rhythm)*, but it's still open to outside influence, and the body is obliged to perform tasks that are not directly the expression of the supreme Impulsion, hence the fatigue, the friction. Yet a supramental body suspended in a world that is not the earth would hardly be a solution, would it! We need something that has the power to resist the contagion. Man can't resist the contagion of the animal—he can't; he is in constant relation with it. So what will that being do? It would seem that for a long time—a long time—the law of contagion will prevail.

(Satprem:) I don't know, I don't see any impossibility there.

(Mother:) No?

(Satprem:) As long as that power of Light is there, I don't see what could touch it.

(Mother:) But the whole world would be crushed! That's it, you see. When That comes, when the Lord is there, there's not one person in a thousand for whom it isn't terrifying. Not in the brain, not in thought—right here, in the flesh. So suppose—suppose it happens—let one being be the condensation and expression, a representation, of the supreme Power, of the supreme Light. What would happen?!

(Satprem:) Well, that's the whole problem.

(Mother:) Yes.

(Satprem:) Because I don't see it as a difficulty

86

of the transformation itself. It seems to be more a difficulty with the world.

(Mother:) If everything could change at the same time, it would be all right, but it's visibly not the case. If one being were transformed all alone ...

(Satprem:) Yes, it would be unbearable, maybe.

(Mother:) Indeed!

(Satprem:) That's perhaps the whole problem. (9/30/66)

The End of Habits

What battle did she not wage! What victory did she not win over the old human habit! It was night and day nonstop.

(Mother:) I have made interesting discoveries. Illnesses, accidents, catastrophes, wars—all that is because the human material consciousness is so small, so narrow that it has a mad taste for drama. The seed of the problem is that smallness, that extreme smallness of the physical consciousness—the material physical consciousness—which has an absolutely perverse taste for drama. Drama—the least thing has to turn into a drama: you have a toothache, it's a drama; you bump into something, it's a drama; two nations are at loggerheads, it becomes a drama—everything becomes a drama. A taste for drama. You have a little bodily disorder, a little thing that should have remained absolutely unnoticed—well, it creates a big hullabaloo, a drama! ... The same teeth that I have had for

87

so long (so long in the same state, that is!), which haven't given me any trouble for years—all of a sudden they, too, have decided it was time to stir up drama! So, raging toothache, swelling—completely and utterly ridiculous!

And that discovery about drama did not come as a thought, you know, not as an observation; it was something acutely experienced, caught as one catches a thief. I caught it. And it's universal, all over the earth. . . . The minute I understood that, it started to quiet down. . . . But death, too, is the result of a taste for drama—what a lovely drama, phew! (6/14/67)

We are making an experiment: finding how to go from the old method to the new one, and so it's . . . The body knows nothing. It is completely ignorant—it has no experience and doesn't know anything; it just has a good will *(Mother opens her hands)*. It has *(laughing)* a number of sensations about what's happening, which are not always very pleasant, and that's all. It doesn't know. It doesn't know the effect—how, why, and all that. Naturally—that is part of what's demanded—it must eat; but in what proportion and how? The transition—how does one make the transition? The pace of the transition, the process of the transition? It knows nothing. This poor body can't say anything because it doesn't know anything. Everything it thought it had learned in ninety years has been clearly proven to be totally worthless *(Mother laughs)*, and now everything has to be learned again. (12/20/69)

In the body (in the cells, in the consciousness of the body) there is a great, constant battle between all the materialistic ideas and the true consciousness, and that creates a ... *(grating gesture)*. In fifteen minutes, everything starts to grate—you're in pain, you feel uncomfortable, as if everything were going to be torn, with unbearable contradictions—and suddenly, with the pressure of the true consciousness, suddenly, brrm! everything disappears in a minute and it becomes ... a marvel. But it isn't something stable: the battle goes on.
But it's truly interesting. (3/7/70)

I had the impression of being all the suffering of the world—all the suffering of the world felt at once.... There is a place, a sort of place, where there is such a dreadful anguish.... Do you hear how difficult it is for me to breathe? That's it. It's constant. It's here *(Mother draws a line across the top of her chest)*. It's here. There's a sort of interdiction to ... *(Mother makes a gesture of rising to join with the Origin above the head)*. As if I absolutely had to find something. ... Strangely, it's from here to here *(gesture from the waist to the knees)*, but mainly here *(waist)*. I can't say what it is, but it's a dreadful anguish. When it comes here *(chest)*, I scream. It's in the legs down to the knees. Now I can hardly walk. It's extremely physical, material. ... I have *absolutely* no doubt that it will be conquered, you understand, but, the point is, has the time come?

. . . That doubt is what's really torturing me.
(9/9/70)

A little body that seemed to embody all human difficulty, all human weight and inertia.

(Mother:) It's the feeling of being constantly between life and death, and the minute you take the right attitude—the minute *the part concerned* takes the right attitude—everything is fine. Quite naturally and easily, everything is fine. It's extraordinary. But it's formidable because there's constant danger. I don't know, maybe a hundred times a day, the sensation of: life or—for the cells, you understand—life or disintegration. And if they tense up, as they usually do, it becomes quite nasty. But they are learning to . . . *(Mother opens her hands in a gesture of abandon).* And then everything is all right. (3/8/72)

It's really curious. At the same time—not one inside the other or one with the other, but one AND the other—at the same time *(Mother puts the fingers of her right hand between the fingers of her left hand)*: a marvel and a horror. Life as it is, as we perceive it in our ordinary consciousness—as it is for humans—seems so . . . dreadful that one wonders how it's possible to live such a thing even for a minute. And the other, AT THE SAME TIME—a marvel. A marvel of light, of consciousness, of power—marvelous! Oh, and a power! . . . It isn't the power of one person *(Mother pinches the skin of her hand)*; it's some-

90

thing—it's something that is everything. You just can't express it. (8/28/71)

There's truly something new—it's *no longer* as it was. All our common sense, our logic, our practical sense—shattered, finished, no more power. No more reality. It no longer corresponds to reality.
It's truly a new world. (5/6/72)

When will we take flight with our true, promised wings? When will we get an earth in the image of our dreams? It isn't Mars or Venus that holds the key to our future, but ourselves, here. One would need to understand what is happening, what was happening inside a little body quietly seated in a remote corner of the globe, a little body staring at a certain point in front of it with a terrifying and pathetic intensity.

(Mother:) **These last few days I've had the feeling, a sort of perception, of a TREMENDOUS power! A power, you know, that seemed capable of reviving a dead person. A tremendous power that uses this *(the body)* without any conscious identification but completely naturally, without —as though there were no resistance. It's a natural condition, and it isn't one thing or another but . . . EVERYTHING *(gesture indicating an immense movement)* that . . . acts according to circumstances. (4/22/70)**

Everything was contained there, in that unwavering look. She was staring at "the problem." Or perhaps, sometimes, the happy azure fields where we will gambol, at last free and light in a physical body.

> *(Mother:)* **There's really something different in the world. Naturally, it will take time to be fully established. That's the battle. From every side, at every level, things are pouring in and externally saying, "Nothing is changed." But that's not true. It isn't true; the body knows it isn't true. Now it knows—it knows the direction. (3/14/70)**

The Resistance

There was "That," and "this." And how does one go from one to the other? The process had begun, that marvelous and so surprising Supramental was there, active on earth, but a human body was still a human body.

> *(Mother:)* **The problem—the problem is that the world is not ready! The substance we are made of *(Mother touches her own body)* partakes of the lack of readiness of the world—of course, since it's the same thing! It's all the same, one and the same thing. There may be in this body a little more light, but so little it's not worth mentioning—it's all the same. . . . Oh, a vile slavery! (2/18/61)**

The system has begun not to want to function in the old way. So what do you do when it comes to eating? Food doesn't have the least attraction

for me—none whatsoever. It seems a completely stupid thing, and yet it "has" to be taken. And the doctors want everything to function as usual —it's impossible. It puts me in a state of—it creates a sort of conflict in the nature. You see, things are going too fast, and at the same time the old nature is resisting—encouraged by doctors and habits. . . . Of course, I can see that if the transformation took place like lightning, it would be terrifying for people. (1/30/71)

A miracle? A glorified body suddenly? But who would be able to bear it? The little humans around Mother were already near exhaustion. They were giving more and more signs of weariness. That Supramental was so strange and contradictory! Mother appeared to be literally melting away, seemingly doomed to increasing physical impotence: she hardly ate, no longer slept at night, and spent all her time seated in her armchair, slightly bent over, staring at the space in front of her—as Sri Aurobindo used to do—or else with her eyes closed, an indefinable expression on her face.

(Mother:) **I am in full transformation; that's why I've lost control. I can no longer do what I used to do. But I see—I see clearly where it's going, but it isn't there yet. So I am not good for anything anymore. This is just interesting from a documentary point of view, because when this phase is over, when the supramental really begins to come, things will change and this will only have a historical value. It's really the transition between two worlds. (8/4/71)**

93

The body feels it no longer belongs to the old way of being, but it knows it isn't in the new way yet; it's still ... It is no longer mortal and not yet immortal. It's quite strange. Quite strange. And sometimes you go from the most dreadful discomfort to ... the marvel—it's strange. An inexpressible bliss. Things are no longer what they were, and they aren't what they are supposed to be. There it is. Strange. (9/18/71)

Sometimes her body whimpered like a child. She no longer spoke, except to Satprem, and everything that "Mother" had stood for in the disciples' understanding had stopped. She spent her time "sleeping," they said.

(Mother:) Yesterday, for some time, I was put in contact with people's thoughts, the way they think. And I saw that I have to be extremely careful—I had better keep quiet because they could easily think that I've become unhinged! You know: "One gets old, there's arteriosclerosis of the brain, one becomes a little stupid, it's the second childhood." I saw it all. It was quite funny! I saw, I was shown a whole way of thinking—and they think they're very clever, very knowledgeable! Anyway.... (7/14/62)

I really think the physical world is changing. It will probably become evident in a few hundred years, because it takes a long time to become visible to the ordinary human consciousness. But the contact is there (Mother feels the air between her fingers), as if ... it were made of something

94

different.

And then, from time to time, something says to me, "Don't say anything! Don't say anything!" I mustn't say a word because people around me would think I am losing my mind. (5/27/72)

They think—they are very polite, very well behaved—but they think: Mother is beginning to . . . she's going down! *(Mother laughs)* All of a sudden (in the middle of doing something or writing or anything at all), all of a sudden, I go into a consciousness in which all the relations are different, and there's a sort of power trying to exert itself. It's very interesting, of course, so instead of continuing what I was doing, I follow the movement—"Look, Mother's falling asleep again!" I read their thoughts as clear as daylight, their reactions, etc. And I am polite; I don't say anything. If I weren't polite, it would create disasters.

But at least one person will know!

. . . I look at this body, and sometimes (when there is too much incomprehension, when those around me are too utterly uncomprehending), it says, "Ah, just let me go." It says to me ("it" is what is still unconscious, too unconscious and not receptive enough), it says, "All right, let me go. Never mind; just let me go." Like that. Not disgusted or tired, just . . . And it's so pitiful. So I say to it *(with a tone as if talking to a child),* "No, no, no."

It's a question of patience, you know. Just a question of patience.

**What is going to happen?
I don't know. We'll see.
In any case, you, for one, will know. You will be
able to tell them** *(laughing)*, **"It isn't as you
think. . . ." I would tell them myself, but they
won't listen to me. (6/15/68)**

**And always the idea that I am o-l-d. I am getting
o-l-d, and of course, for them my consciousness
must be half clouded. They don't have faith,
that's the sum and substance of it. (2/27/71)**

The Forced Departure

They had had enough. Enough of that impossible Supramental Sri Aurobindo had promised for so long, which
had apparently "descended" in 1956 and kept drawing ec-
static and rapturous comments from Mother, but which
nobody ever saw. Where were the "miracles" of the Supramental, the new man as promised by Sri Aurobindo, the
sunlit transformation? There was just a great weariness in
their minds, bad moods, ceaseless quarrels here and there—
a lot of little muffled explosions. They had waited all this
time, exercised immeasurable patience and good will for
that Supramental—they had "given their life" for it. For
what result? Was not this another tall tale, a dream for the
next millennium? And Mother, silent in her armchair and
staring. . . .

It had to stop.

They decided to hasten events. The most headstrong
among them took the initiative. First, communications had
to stop with the only human element who understood what

Mother was trying to do in the silence of her room, who was not deceived by the apparent contradiction of her condition, the only one who did not think her old or crazy.

(*Mother:*) Fortunately I keep silent—I only speak to you—otherwise they would surely say, "Mother's unhinged!" (4/22/70)

I have to be careful when I am with people, otherwise they might think I am going crazy! (9/18/71)

My child, you're the only person I can say this to—there's nobody, not one person! No one who could even understand. And that increases the difficulty, because I am constantly weighed down by the stupidity of people's thoughts (stupidity in the sense that they don't understand), the thoughts of all those around me, who think that I—what *they* call "I" is not me!—am sick and that ... I can't say anything! (4/6/63)

Satprem had to be removed because his support only helped prolong and justify an impossible and incomprehensible situation. It was not easy to "see" a new being and a new species in that little body increasingly short of breath. So, one day, as he was about to enter Mother's room as usual, Satprem found the door closed: "Mother is sick. She can't see anybody." Mother was "sick." It was straightforward and simple. Even the doctor agreed.

(*Mother:*) I have nothing to do with an illness from which one recovers! I can't recover!—it's a

work of transformation. All this way of thinking, feeling, reacting really belongs to another world —really another world.... To the point that, if I didn't respect people's peace of mind, I would say, "I'm not sure I'm alive or dead." Because there is a life, a type of life vibration, that is totally independent of—no, let me put it this way: the way people ordinarily perceive life, feel that they are alive, is intimately connected to a certain perception they have of themselves, a perception of their body and themselves; now, suppress that perception entirely, that type of perception, that type of relation people call "I am alive"—suppress it—how can you say, "I am alive" or "I am not alive"? It NO LONGER EXISTS. ... So what they call "I am alive" ... I can't say "I am alive" as they do. It's something totally different. (6/12/62)

I am surrounded, you see, by people who think I am sick and treat me like a sick person. And I know I am not sick. But everything, absolutely everything is demolished, in disorder. (5/16/70)

And of course, what's a nuisance is that people don't know anything, don't understand anything, even the ones who see me all the time, like the doctor, for instance. (2/18/61)

The scenario then unfolded very quickly. Deprived of any human support and understanding, completely isolated from the outside world, treated with powerful drugs and guarded night and day by her close attendants, Mother managed to hold out for another six months. And one day she left. On November 17, 1973, her heart simply stopped. Now she was making sense again! A stiff little body on a white sheet—this is concrete and reassuringly human. Death, indeed, makes sense. They were going to make her into a saint, organize a funeral worthy of her greatness, with a beautiful coffin in rosewood, placed next to Sri Aurobindo's beneath the flower-covered slab. They had picked up the trail again. Sri Aurobindo and Mother were back. And everybody felt so close to them, so full of emotion while watching that coffin, carried by six pairs of arms. . . .

The End of the Story?

So the curtain falls. The story is over. All those hundreds of hours of recorded conversations with Satprem, all the words she spoke, where she alluded to something quite different from a little death at the end of the road, that Hope she spelled out day after day—gone, forgotten, another fairy tale? Death has the last word as usual and everything comes to a stop? And, as usual, the only choice of the living is between a new church and disbelief?

Well, not exactly.

Indeed, that would be really to misjudge the Supramental and forget what Sri Aurobindo had so often repeated. To begin with, it is not to create another teaching or external movement that Sri Aurobindo had toiled all those years (nor to do miracles), but to bring upon the earth a new principle of consciousness, another way of living life (and death). He had done his work thoroughly, honestly: he had prepared the ground, drawn down the new seed, watched day after day over the first tender roots. . . . For her part, Mother had grown a first plant above the ground and in the open air of everyday life, established a firm root system that withstood earthly conditions. Sri Aurobindo and Mother had demonstrated that a truly new life was possible on earth. What more could we ask? There only remained to try it. The living had a third choice after all.

(Sri Aurobindo:) **It is not intended to supramentalise humanity at large, but to establish the principle of the supramental consciousness in the earth-evolution. If that is done, all that is needed will be evolved by the supramental power itself. It is not therefore important that the mission should be widespread. What is important is that the thing should be done at all in however small a number; that is the only difficulty. (22:11)**

(Mother:) **I don't know, but it seems to be the first time that the instrument, instead of being intended to bring the "News," the "Revelation," the spark, has been intended to ... to realize— to do the work, the hidden labor. And indeed, it acknowledges it, but it doesn't blissfully go into the joy of that acknowledgement, and every minute, *despite what is done*, it is forced to see how much work remains to be done! So the body will only rejoice when the work is done. What does it mean, "the work done"? It means something ESTABLISHED. (11/15/67)**

It is now up to us humans to take over, to understand what they have done and follow the marks and signposts they have left. After all, a new world, a new way of being on earth, is worth some effort. Unless we wish to continue in the old way? It's always a possibility. The choice is entirely ours. That, they cannot do for us. A little commitment is necessary on our part.

Mother is gone, of course, but she had fully accomplished her task. She stayed until the last minute, the extreme limit. And it is truly because the incomprehension around her was too absolute that she decided to leave. She could as well have stayed indefinitely, one could say, for she had found the secret of *overlife*.

(Mother:) **The step that humanity must take *immediately* is to overcome exclusivism once and for all. To be supple enough and wide enough to combine everything together. This is what I keep knocking against these days, in every domain—every domain.... In the body, too. The body has the habit of: "This and not that, this OR that, this or that...." No, no, no—this AND that. The great division, you know: life versus death. That's the long and the short of it. And everything is a consequence of that. Well—words are stupid, but—*overlife* is life AND death together.** (1/3/70)

You see, it isn't that death disappears (death as we conceive of it, as we know it, and as compared to life as we know it)—it isn't like that, not like that at all. BOTH are in the process of changing ... into something we still don't know, which seems both extremely dangerous and totally marvelous. Dangerous, because the slightest

101

wrong move has frightfully serious consequences. And marvelous. This is the consciousness, the true consciousness of immortality—it isn't "immortality" as we conceive of it; it's something else. We tend to want certain things to be true (what we perceive as favorable) and others to disappear—it doesn't work that way! It doesn't work that way. It's that EVERYTHING becomes different. (7/12/72)

We will very much miss her silvery laughter. If she were here, we could walk hand in hand toward a happier world. But she is not far—just behind the paper-thin veil of our material consciousness—and who knows if one day she will not appear to our physical gaze, unsealed at last?

And this is where the existence and research of Satprem take on their full meaning. Mother said it repeatedly: he was the only one who really understood and followed her, the only person who did not politely swallow the official version of Mother's death. To run counter to such an ... overwhelmingly concrete fact is not an easy task: "Am I not crazy? Or just plain dreaming?" Indeed, it is insane to challenge the combined wisdom of such a respectable and spiritual pack. It takes courage and perhaps more than courage. The battle that Satprem had to go through after Mother's departure in order to preserve the *Agenda* and publish it integrally, despite all the obstacles "fraternally" strewn beneath his footsteps, is on a par with the best James Bond. One day, the story of that fight will be interesting to relate. But in the meantime—and that is what primarily counts—we are engaged in the second stage of the Experience: the human stage. Are humans going to realize that the world has changed in its foundations? Today's world is as cataclysmic and dangerous as can be; all sorts of worldwide catastrophes seem to loom over us. Will they have to manifest with full force for us to understand that the human world is finished in its present mental form, that it *must* mutate to something else or perish? There is that "other" possibility—in the cells—which would thrust us into such a new and surprising world, where all the old cataclysmic ghosts no longer have any place, a world of absolute spontaneity, infinite peace, eternal youth.... But the old ghosts still seem to have a lot of attraction for the human consciousness. Which one will win? It's almost like a race. It would take very little to tip the scales: a few human eyes opening up, and . . .

Such is the challenge and such is the meaning of the first man to try to follow Sri Aurobindo's and Mother's footsteps in the cellular consciousness of a human body. All is still possible and open because that man is trying. Will we understand his words? Time is perhaps shorter than we think.

PART THREE

SATPREM

Let Us Try. . .

A mind absolved from life, made calm to know,
A heart divorced from the blindness and the pang,
The seal of tears, the bond of ignorance,
He turned to find that wide world-failure's cause.[1]

TO EFFECT evolution, we need to be in contact with our body. We are never in contact with our body—or if we are, it is always through a series of more or less distorting filters, a whole vertical structure we call ourselves: our thoughts, feelings, sensations and many reactions to life's stimuli. We "think" our body sick because the symptoms fit the description in Merck's Manual; we "feel" that such and such a pain indicates a worsening of the situation; we "fear" cancer and we are "afraid" of dying—in the end it's always death. But what does our *body* think? And how can we know what it thinks—or, rather, what it really goes through—as long as we think for it, feel for it, and fear the worst for it (always the worst, to be sure)? All that automatic, reactive buzz, all those "layers" of human habit which hem our body in an implacable web of ready-made truths and pre-concluded conclusions must stop interfering. They have to fall silent. The body must be left on its own in

---

1. Sri Aurobindo, *Savitri*, p. 202.

107

order to express its own possibilities, normally shrouded and appropriated by all the "higher" mental and vital activities. Left to itself, the body will reveal its secrets. If it is divine, built divinely, those divine traits *must* then manifest themselves. It's a risky game, perhaps mortal. But as we shall see, the basic postulate is correct: the body *is* divine. Left on its own, it shows it in an astonishing and miraculous way (we are just not used to these miracles, while for the body they are completely natural).

The Breakthrough

This is how Satprem describes, in one of his most recent letters, the battle to break through those layers of mental habit that cover us.

"The New World is not an escape—it is a conquest. A difficult conquest, more difficult than the conquest of the Sahara desert or the ascent of Mount Everest = they are child's play. I am not in the habit of exaggerating. And if you cannot fight your battle now, right where you are, you will not be able to fight it later—it is now that you pass the test (or don't pass it).

". . . And it does become dangerous, for the New World will not tolerate one second of deception, not one grain of falsehood—otherwise you don't pass; it throws you out and it can be absolutely ruthless. In the old days, they spoke of 'dragons' and 'serpents' that guarded the 'Treasure'—it is a picturesque translation of a real fact. You do not cheat with the dragon: if you are not pure, you get burned. Therefore, your battle of purity, of sincerity, of honesty, of true and divine simplicity, must be waged now, or else you will be thrown out, and the second time might be worse than the first. One does not approach these serious and grave things without danger—though it's only dangerous for insincerity and impurity.

". . . What, then, is this battle all about? It is quite simple. We know the general system of the world— rather, a few know it: those who have tried to get out of it. That System is cruel: there are implacable and very nasty forces lying in wait at every street corner for the 'lawbreaker,' and if you break the law, the Sordid begins to show its teeth. But as long as you march in step, the Sordid gives you broad and charming smiles. It is called Justice, Poetry, Religion, Ideal—it takes on every mask to hide the real story, the sordid story. Personally, I was brutally freed from the masks at the age of twenty[1]—I have been a lawbreaker for 40 years. I know the trade well.

"So, when you are courageous and a little obstinate, you get out of the System. That is the easiest and 'fun' part of the Battle. You are 'against'—it's simple. You stand 'apart'—it's simple (not always so simple). But then, if you are honest and sincere with yourself, you quickly realize (more or less quickly) that the System has its roots within, right inside your own flesh. The Sordid is cozily inside and holds you by a thousand invisible little strings, which sway you this way and that. This is beginning to be far less amusing and far more difficult, because the Sordid, the System, then begins to show its teeth inside—there, I can assure

---

1. In Nazi concentration camps, where Satprem spent a year and a half for belonging to the French Resistance.

you, it takes a lot of heroism not to let yourself be eaten up. One can be eaten up by pulling the wool over one's eyes and fantasizing about oneself. You are then no longer dealing with nice little cops, quite becoming in their easily recognizable uniform, but with cruel, universal forces, which hold the entire human world in prison—you are the prime keeper of your own jail. There, as I have learned myself, you must be very strong, that is, very *pure*—purity is the *only* force. To overwhelm the Dragon, there is no other weapon than purity.

"Hence the New World means uprooting the System from *within* oneself. And ultimately, the System has roots right down into the genetic code and in each cell, because we are the son of the father who was the son of the great-grandfather who was . . . All the holy Church is there, and all the holy Horror. Do you understand the magnitude of the battle?

"So if you are still at the stage of whipping out the machine gun, of banging your fist on the table, writing poetry, and saying 'me,' you are entirely beside the point and entirely the puppet of those cruel forces— you will write the poetry of Revolt and the novel of the glorious 'me,' which is but a ridiculous little marionette. For those forces, revolt is as good as surrender, evil as fine as good, love (so-called) as tantalizing and delectable as hate. They are the two masks of the Sordid. And the 'me' is the toothsome little puppet of those forces. You get out of that horrid System when you begin to throw that famous 'me' out the window, because, at any rate, that 'me' is merely the 'me' of the grandfather, the great-grandfather and all the holy Tribe—you must get out of the Tribe once and for all.

"... I could tell you a little story. It happened more than 25 or 30 years ago. I was in Ceylon (it was another world, then), in the south of Ceylon, in a village on the edge of the jungle. I lived in the temple, slept in the temple, and every day I begged for my food with my copper pot—at that time I thought I was out of the System! I was usually given rice mixed with sliced green pepper. That pepper was so hot that it burned my fingers when I ate my rice. Finally, since I had already contracted typhus in the camps and amoebic dysentery, I started to purge blood every day. I was very sick, but I went on with the same diet anyway because I'm stubborn. And one day, as I was washing my copper pot along the river bank, I started to indulge in self-pity, saying to myself, 'Here you are at the end of the world (there was still an 'end of the world,' then), with nothing, and you're croaking.' In other words, I was spinning pitiable yarns for my own benefit, but, still, I was in a rather bad way. Then all of a sudden, on the bank of that river, while I was washing my copper pot and holding in my aching guts, a Force came over me, literally seized me and shouted into my ears, 'But what does it matter *what you think!*'

"I tell you, a mask fell off me. Suddenly I was no longer the same: what I thought did not matter in the least. Everything we think is a fairy tale; it's FAKE. A total, unmitigated lie. Dysentery is a lie, typhus is a lie, cancer is a lie, everything is a lie—everything we think is false and fake. There is SOMETHING ELSE.

"This is the first mask that falls: the mask of the mind.

"Then there is a second mask: the mask of the wonderful and eternal sentiments that fill human beings. This one is a far more deceptive and tougher mask: I 'love,' I 'feel'—oh, all that holy tribe of passions and desires and hurt feelings and 'I feel . . .'! Yet they are nothing but sordid little strings pulled by the same cruel forces. So there, too, you must reach the point of the cry: 'But what does it matter *what I feel!*' And a whole set of theatrics falls.

"Not easy.

"Once that second mask—the vital mask—falls off, you are very near what I would call the 'burning Zero.' In other words, there is nothing left; everything is broken, *unmasked*—you are naked and ridiculous and nothing whatsoever. Then it begins burning inside. That is, it begins to BE—something that is neither the grandfather nor the great-grandfather, neither poetry nor religion nor ideal nor anything of the whole damn sordid story. Something that IS—without words, pure, simple as a fire or a child. You are the child of the fire. You are the burning nothing. You ARE.

"This is the beginning.

"Afterwards, you have to go on uprooting the other falsehoods in the depths of the body, in the cells—that is the last part of the battle." *(letter from Satprem to a brother, June 1983)*

This breakthrough, this descent to the cellular level, takes, of course, several years—a very short time considering the millennia of human habits involved. It requires courage, but especially a lot of patience and endurance. And it is readily done in the midst of everyday life. Indeed, one *must* live a normal life to do it, for it is life itself that provides at every instant the opportunity to measure one's own progress, the degree of stillness of the various parts of the being: as long as there are reactions to one thing or another, it means that that particular point is not conquered, not silenced—EVERYTHING must come to a stop.

In Satprem's case, this descent must have taken place unknown to all (except him!), while Mother was still in her body, confiding her experiences to him, then, after her departure, while he was engaged in a very "external" and fierce battle to publish the *Agenda*. In 1982, all 13 volumes of the *Agenda* having been duly published down to the last comma, Satprem suddenly found himself before a terrible wall. He had finished all his external work: he had written all the books that he had to, the hundreds of letters that he had to; he had extended unceasing encouragement to this one and that one, and his sweet smile, which dispelled all our little clouds in a second. What was there left to do? A man, in a physical body, must *do* something. The fire burning in his heart was telling him that surely he could not go on writing books and letters till doomsday. He had done it, and it had become another routine, obviously pleasant for the recipients—but he had perhaps something better to do?

Let Us Try

Thus, gradually, *from within*, from that rather strange condition of inner stillness in which he lived came the need to go farther down, right into the body, as Mother and Sri Aurobindo had done. This was in May 1982.

" . . . What was just an 'idea' or a conjecture (transformation) has become the one pressing and imperative need. I don't know anything about it; all I know is that there is an imperative, inevitable, irreversible aspiration, as it were, and it has become a sort of physical necessity, a groping need, and I will not be able to do anything else. I have no idea of the direction to take, or where I am going, but in a sense it does not really matter; what matters is that one-pointed concentration and the unfolding of an almost physical need, which holds or must hold its own ineluctable direction. There is a kind of awakening of the aspiration in the physical consciousness, and it moves according to its own unknown laws (unknown to me). All I know is that I want to live exclusively in that. All I mentally and almost physically know is the necessity of producing one first earthly sample of the new species—of taking one first step, of materializing one first possibility as a concrete and realizable hope for those other human beings who have the potential. The earth needs a concrete hope and a clear sign of its next course—so all can say, even if they cannot yet be it: this is where we are going. It is the only obvious thing to do, even if it is impossible. What would have appeared to me before as a kind of unbounded ambition has become a simple and indisputable fact. I don't care in the least about being the 'first sample,' but it has to take place somewhere on the earth, in a first human who will put his body at the disposal of . . . 'that.' I don't care whether I succeed or not, and in a way it is none of my business; my business is to try to the utmost. It is possible, even probable, that other unknown people are attempting to do the same thing in their own way, with a different vocabulary or in a different form, but the evolutionary drive is ineluctable and imperative, and it seizes all those who are willing to put themselves 'at the disposal of.' Whatever may happen to others, I feel impelled to follow this path, without the least 'personal' overtone—actually, you no longer have any idea where the 'I' is in that groping darkness, where your only hope is the divine Hand, if it cares to take mine. The only new capital and simple fact that happened is that one day (it was May 14), I felt something saying yes. That and the aspiration in the physical consciousness are the only two driving forces in something that looks otherwise totally dark.

". . . The appearance of a first sample of the divine species on earth is ineluctable. And it can be *anyone*; the main thing is that our aspiration should carry that 'anyone' to his divine destination. The enterprise is certain. By withdrawing, Mother and Sri Aurobindo wanted to leave to the human being the grace or favor of taking the first step of his own evolution and passing through the gates They opened. Satprem is just one aspirant among others, and with or without him the work will be done and a first terrestrial sample will inevitably be born to the divine life." *(letter from Satprem to Luc, May 1982)*

Simultaneously, Satprem decided to withdraw from public view, along with his companion, Sujata, not to enjoy a well-deserved peace and realization away from worldly life, but to devote himself more exclusively to that ultimate battle in the roots of life. A total concentration was necessary, for, at that level, the least mistake can be fatal; no "slip" is permitted when it comes to the functioning of the cells—we depend too much on them.

LIFE WITHOUT DEATH

The Double Mooring

From that "strategic" retreat, he sent some rare, essential news about the new phase he was engaged in:

"I want to tell you a 'dream' I had some time ago, which is one of the landmarks in the story since Mother left. It is actually the continuation and conclusion of that vision I had immediately after Mother left, in which I saw a great crevice in the desert and me lying flat over it (with my bicycle on my back!) to make a bridge or join with the other side of the crevice. I nearly completely missed the vision I am about to tell you, but I had an experience that suddenly made me realize the meaning and importance of what I had seen. These are not visions; they are actions.

"This is what I noted down in my notebook under the date of March 21 (spring equinox):

"I remember that two nights ago, that is, during the night of the 18th to the 19th, I saw something that now makes sense: I was aboard a rather large boat (not a sailboat, I don't think), and we were about to dock and moor the boat alongside the quay. The boat was still moving and I could see the big steel cable moored to a bitt, but that cable was unwinding, and the boat began to leave the quay without casting off its mooring, moving slowly away from the coast. Then we passed by a beautiful, all-white building standing in the distance, all alone in the middle of the sea (on second thought, it may have been a temple, but very clean, very white, very harmonious, standing roughly halfway). Finally, the boat reached the other shore or other side (side of what, I don't know, and I can't say I saw

116

a 'shore,' but it was the 'other side' of the first quay, to which we were still moored). And we moored on that second side, too, with a big steel cable. I thought to myself, 'Well, well, this is a double mooring.'

"I cannot describe the boat because I was too busy maneuvering it, nor could I see who was on board, but there seemed to be a few people, not many. This was the side one disembarked on. What was most prominent in my consciousness was that 'double mooring' and the big steel cable that connected us with the first quay.

"To sum up, both sides are connected with a big cable and you do not leave the mooring of one to travel to the other. It is a double mooring.

"I think the first quay stands for the earth and the other quay, for the supramental world. The white building at midway must be the world of the gods and religions.

"Well, it looks like we are coming to land." *(letter from Satprem to Luc, April 1983)*

The New

The vision is quite clear: Satprem had made the junction, the "double mooring," between the terrestrial shore—bodily matter—and the supramental shore "up above." Like Sri Aurobindo, like Mother, his cells were directly in contact with the higher Fire—without any intermediary. Freed of all the distorting and asphyxiating layers, his bodily substance was directly imbibing the Consciousness-Force that moves the universe—an astronaut without a space suit, you might say! What was going to happen?

"Somehow, I feel a necessity to take stock of the situation—never mind if the stock is still incomplete. To mentalize things only muddies them, like putting a lid between yourself and 'the thing.'

"Actually, I could boil down my entire discourse to a fortuitous and insignificant little experience that happened recently. I met X and asked him somewhat mechanically, 'What's new?' And at that very moment, something in me stopped, looked up, smiled and said (it was not me saying it), 'The New is here.'

"That is the fact.

"I have therefore spent a whole year in concentration. It was on May 14, 1982, that I sat down and said to myself, 'Let us try.' And it was on May 13, 1983, that I was abruptly torn out of that concentration to go to R. This was a difficult exercise and a 'test.'

" . . . But the fact, the other fact, is that the moment the plane took off for R., a tremendous power seized hold of me—the kind I experienced during my solitary concentrations—and literally doubled me up and did not leave me—in the train, the streets, the car and everywhere. It was so extraordinarily dense that I said to Sujata, sitting next to me, 'But don't you feel this?' (the impression was that it could smash and flatten just about anything). And the funny thing is, Sujata replied, 'Yes, I feel a relaxation in my whole body.' I was like an electrical power station and she was relaxing! (I now understand why.) What is most extraordinary is that nobody seems to feel it. It is an incredible power, unbearable for the human norm, yet it seems as transparent as air. I don't know, but if you transposed that power to the vital level, it would blow up everything it went through (and if you transposed it to the mental level, it would explode the brain). And yet it's like air! But what is supremely interesting is that this power is bearable (humanly bearable) only at the level of MATTER—but a purified matter, otherwise it also explodes (that is, any obstacle or cover-up explodes; there is a whole 'adjustment' and process of purification to undergo, first—that's been the work for the last year). The supreme intensities of the Spirit are bearable only at the level of matter . . . as if they were the same thing. And anything in between is falsehood.

"That opens up new horizons.

"The fact, then, is that that Power is now *established*. This was the difficult exercise.

"I cannot tell you in two pages what has happened during the last year. But I did manage to keep a diary where the daily stages are objectively recorded—one day it may be useful, unless the Experience takes place *in vivo* and physically, in which case it will be visible, as Mother would say, and we won't need a 'diary'! But it is taking place. How far will it go? I don't know, but it has begun.

"The one last fact I wanted to mention to you is something quite surprising, which has happened hundreds of times, and which is a real discovery for me. It is really 'my' discovery. I don't know how to say it in simple terms because it is new (except for Sri Aurobindo and Mother, and maybe the Vedic Rishis, nobody has seen it before, and Mother and Sri Aurobindo have not even mentioned it explicitly anywhere—at least I am not aware of it). In order for you to understand the 'fact,' I have to backtrack a little:

"The first stage of this supramental yoga is the awakening of the aspiration in the material consciousness, the body-consciousness. I need not tell you what that is. As a result of this aspiration, 'That' descends, the supramental descends. And that's a marvel—a rather frightening marvel at the beginning—but a marvel the likes of which you have never seen! It takes months to accustom the body to that cataract (it's more like molten ore), because all the intermediate layers have to be purified. Any obstruction blows up or threatens to blow up everything; the least speck of dust has 'explosive' effects. It is long and difficult to withstand, and absolutely marvelous. Thus, 'That' descends and grinds (does it ever!) and churns and purifies all the intermediate magma. This is the first 'line' between the human material consciousness and the supramental Consciousness. Then, one day, you enter the second stage (or third, rather), and this is where I made my discovery.

"As a result of those repeated 'descents,' one day, suddenly, the whole MATERIAL consciousness, the BODY-CONSCIOUSNESS, starts to rise! This is totally unheard of! We have heard of (or felt) the Kundalini rising. It's something I have experienced thousands and thousands of times for so many years. It rises above and blossoms out into a vast and very luminous and pleasant expanse—and so on and so forth. But here, all of a sudden, one day, it's as if (not 'as if') the body were under a gigantic magnet and the whole consciousness OF THE BODY starts to rise. (You feel millions of minuscule particles caught by the 'magnet' and starting to rise from everywhere at once.) The first time, you have absolutely the impression of dying—

120

this is the 'way out' when one dies. And for quite a long time, every day the body feels it is about to die. It is a feeling difficult to overcome; it's difficult not to 'let go.' But then, the higher it rises (truly, peak after peak after peak), the more you feel that, instead of a rarefied air, you are going through dense layers, denser and denser, almost unbearable—it almost reaches the breaking point, as if that *material body-consciousness* entered a molten atmosphere 'up there.' And this is where, after days and weeks of 'adaptation,' something quite surprising happened: you rose and rose under the attraction of that magnet and it felt denser and denser, and suddenly, without any explanation, it was right THERE. You were no longer ascending or descending—it was THERE. It was right in the body, at the level of matter, without high or low—that same density of atmosphere or power was directly and immediately there. It's like a sudden reversal: you have arrived. As if you had spent days and days climbing to heaven, and all of a sudden that heaven above was right in front of you, in your bedroom and in your everyday body! You feel a little stupid. You are wide-eyed—but there it is.

"I can find explanations after the fact, but the supremely interesting point (what I call 'my' discovery) is that the *material body-consciousness* is what rises and joins with the Supramental. I had always wondered about that supramental consciousness that one draws from 'above' and about that supramental plane located 'above,' and I had often asked Mother, 'But how and why above? It should rather be found below, by going down instead of up.' Indeed, I could not understand how the Kundalini or the mental consciousness or the vital consciousness or the 'spiritual' consciousness—or any form of consciousness we know—could possibly establish a contact with the Supramental. I found it illogical that the mind, even at its highest levels, should make the connection with the Supramental—you might as well ask the old fish to make the connection with the lizard without leaving its higher spiritual fish consciousness! And Mother had never clearly answered my question. She was always saying (like Sri Aurobindo) that one had *first* to find the Supramental above—what she did not say is that you have to find it with the *material* consciousness, the BODY-CONSCIOUSNESS! Have you ever heard of the material consciousness rising! Well, it is a fact: it rises. You even feel, underneath, that you are about to die. Mother had said it: 'The body is the bridge.' But have you ever heard of a body rising above to find the Supramental? Well, the contradiction is now resolved (for me).[1]

"My explanation after the fact may be awkward, but I am going to try anyway. There is that sudden reversal: all of a sudden, it's right *there*; what you were actually searching for up above, that interminable climb

---

1. To clarify this last paragraph, Satprem was later asked about a conversation he had with Mother on January 24, 1961 (excerpted in part 2 of this book), in which she clearly says, "The consciousness rose, rose, rose—rose until . . . the junction took place. . . . And it was the consciousness of *the body*." This is what he replied:

"Yes, later, much later I remembered that experience of Mother's and asked myself if it was not the same thing. But what people don't understand is the enormous difference between the schoolboy hearing about the Amazon and the person suddenly thrust face to face with the Oyapock River—you may well tell him, 'Look, that's exactly what you read on page 372 of your geography book'; he will shake his head and say, 'Well, maybe, but it's still not the same thing!'"

through denser and denser layers suddenly ends on a puzzling and mystifying little window. It's *there*; you're in it, as if you had never risen! You climb to heaven for hours and days—to end up finding heaven on earth (and on your two feet)! What does it all mean? (I really opened my eyes wide; I mean, I opened my eyes right in the middle of the experience to touch my body and make sure I was not dreaming or 'spiritualizing.') Finally, I seemed to understand this: you 'rise,' that is to say, the body-consciousness rises to go *through* the fishbowl; it traverses all the layers covering matter—and it gets denser and denser as you get near the most external peels or the most external crust—then, all of a sudden, the body-consciousness finds itself again; it *finds itself again* in the Supramental as though it had never left it! Heaven is in matter, all the way down in matter. All the intermediate layers (mental, vital, etc.) are what makes a gangue or cocoon of falsehood difficult to break through. But once that is broken through, matter is *itself* again, that is, divine! It is perfectly divine without high or low. It has never ceased being divine; it's only that 'plug' of men-

---

"One truly understands only when one is 'on the scene.' And then it's brand new. Therefore, I apologize to Mother, to Sri Aurobindo, and to the Vedic rishis, in all humility; and I have to admit I did not understand anything until it happened to me. And I invite my exegete friends to leave the page 372 and to take a 'direct' trip on the Oyapock River."

Later, Satprem added the following:

"To be more precise, when Mother told me that experience, I had not clearly understood what she meant. I thought it was the *Kundalini*, since she said that later 'it' came down from center to center. But in what I experienced (for weeks, day after day and for hours on end), it was the *whole body* that rose; there was no 'Kundalini,' or else the whole body was the Kundalini! It was a total mass."

tal and vital dirt that prevents the whole Current from being wholly and divinely itself. The body-consciousness 'rises' through the layers and suddenly finds itself again!

"Thus, one understands that everything can be done and everything is possible.

"This is exactly my vision of the 'double mooring': you do not leave the earthly, material mooring to moor to the supramental quay. It's a double mooring. The 'journey' is the crossing of the layers. Once they are crossed, there is only one quay and one earth—but a true earth!

"The 'New' is *here*!

"There remains to do a long and slow (?) and thorough cleansing of all the cells and atoms—so 'That' can flow unobstructed. Then EVERYTHING WILL BE POSSIBLE.

"But the passage is made. It is open. And it is open for everybody. Mother's 'web' is an absolute reality: if one point opens up, everything opens up for everybody. They have made a hole in the web. I can testify to it. Who wants to go through?

"And I understand why Sujata felt a 'relaxation' when I felt like a nuclear reactor! She was herself again!" *(letter from Satprem to Luc, April 1983)*

Satprem had reached the site of the work. At that fundamental level, there was no distance, no time, no distinction between bodies. Everything was ONE. He stood in the very heart of the world, at the tenuous origin where things are born. And he was also in the midst of a formidable energy, terrifying for a little human body—the very Energy of creation. One cannot even imagine what it is. But there, at least, one was no longer dreaming or pleasantly spiritualizing; one was right before THE Thing, and no nonsense.

The real miracle, the astonishing marvel is that this should be at all possible at the human level of things, which always appears to us so frail and impotent. Actually, it is all those muddy layers that hold us in their heavy shackles of impossibility and weakness! On its own, matter is all-powerful; it is totally divine and made in the very image of the energy that created the universe. Only a sort of sticky illusion prevents us from realizing it—let us wipe the illusion out of our bodies and lives, and we will be before Reality.

But what does one *do* exactly at that level of absolute power. What is the task of the pioneer confronted with the "original egg"?

Two years had passed since Satprem had withdrawn from the world to be closer to the world. We were now in the spring of 1984. A meeting was arranged without any guarantee that he would be able to speak of his work. One does not "speak" of these things. Throughout the ages, those who have truly contributed to the earth's welfare in the silence of their heart have done so without words; actions speak for themselves, in the language of life. What is at stake here, though, is human evolution, a possibility opened in principle for every human being. And Satprem has always been willing to share his experiences, in the hope that a word here or there might help someone to grasp the truth of his or her being, to seize a little of the Reality hidden beneath the appearance of the outer personality.

(Sri Aurobindo:) No one is a god, but each man has a god within him. To manifest him is the aim

of the divine life. That everyone can do. I admit
that certain individuals have greater or lesser
capacities.... But whatever the capacity, if once
God places His finger upon a man and his spirit
awakes, greater or lesser and all the rest make
little difference. The difficulties may be more, it
may take more time, what is manifested may not
be the same—but even this is not certain. The
god within takes no account of all these difficulties and deficiencies; he forces his way out. Were
there few defects in my mind and heart and life
and body? Few difficulties? Did it not take time?
Did God hammer at me sparingly—day after
day, moment after moment? Whether I have become a god or something else I do not know. But
I have become or am becoming something—
whatever God desired. This is sufficient. And it
is the same with everybody. *(letter from Sri
Aurobindo to his younger brother, April 7, 1920)*

Uprooting Death

Satprem had greatly changed since I had last seen him.
Something indefinable in his look betrayed the new intensity he was living in day after day. He was totally "present,"
with even a mischievous little gleam in his eye, and light-
years away at the same time, as if his body were a bridge
between some infinite dimension where the worlds are
created and the immediate space in front of us. Something
inexpressible around him, like great wings of infinite soft-
ness, reminded one of Mother—it was there without words,
concretely—but if one looked too probingly or tried to "un-

derstand," everything vanished. One had to be soft oneself, to let the great wings enfold one without thought or understanding. Then, after a while, one "understood," but in a different way: the understanding came from within, with a soft heat, and one knew: "Yes, this is *it*."

Several days passed. Sometimes, in the evening, Satprem would invite me to accompany him on his walk in the countryside. We would sit in silence under the trees, and everything would stop except for that life of life kindled within the being and illuminating everything with its rays of knowledge and peace. The world around unfolded divinely. One day, however, he had broken the silence: "In this business, you spend your time dying without dying!" That had slipped out of him, perhaps because he had felt my silent questions beside him. But he could not or would not say more. There were so many things implied in that little sentence, a whole mysterious and dangerous world, that I was left speechless.

Abruptly, a few days later, after inviting me to accompany him, Satprem added, "You might as well take your tape recorder—one never knows!" We walked some distance in silence, sat down before a lovely expanse of green. I pressed the button:

(Satprem:) The whole work is actually to . . . try to build, to fabricate the base of that transitional being—that being who is still human and will make . . . I don't know . . . the transition to the supramental man, who will no longer be animal, no longer driven in the animal way.

That's the work Mother was doing.

I don't know what will happen, but what I understand—I can only talk about what I understand at this time, through my experience—is that the whole task is to . . . UPROOT

127

death. One could say, the FRAUD of death. But it isn't a mental fraud; it goes right down to the roots of life—to the very first claws of life in matter, as it were, to the ROOTS, what we call the roots of life. Well, you actually realize that the roots of life are the roots of death—they are the same thing.

(silence)

It's a real labor to reach that point and realize that . . . You see, what they call "death" is nothing; it's just the end result, but you realize what a CRUEL domination has seized hold of all life—at least human life. It's a cruel, dreadful, horrible domination. It's . . . abominable. And that's the CRUEL DOMINATION over life in matter.

So, in a way, the whole work is to EXPOSE that.

But, of course, this doesn't take place in your head—you expose it after you've managed not to die from it! And then, you face it a thousand times, ten thousand times, a hundred thousand times, every second, for hours, and every day.

That's what the work is all about, you see, in a way to . . . EXPOSE THIS FRAUD, this falsehood that wants us to believe that it rules, that it is life.

Death wants us to believe that *it* is life.

But the moment you start uprooting the fraud (all this takes place in the body, you understand; it's in the body), well, you also uproot . . . it makes you believe: "You see, you're dying! You're dying! Your heart will stop and your brain will give out and . . . " That's what happens. You are made to see this, feel this, in *thousands* of ways.

So the whole work is to . . . (Of course, you can't possibly do it, do this work, so long as the other Force is not there. How could you do that with your own forces? How could you even go down at that level without the other Power?) So it's like a ... battle, I don't know, between that cruel domination which wants you to believe—and has very powerful means to make you believe!—that it is not at all an illusion, that it rules and that ... Look, *this* is life, and if you start fooling with it, you're simply going to croak! It can be very convincing when it wants to.

But it's a fraud!

It's a lie.

What we call life is DEATH!

And it's as though the body had millions of fibers planted in an old evolutionary soil, an old evolutionary soil that is human, that is—well, it's "life," and if you pull out the roots, it'll just die!

So you must pull out the roots and then *turn* them around toward true life—true life, which is *without* death—PURE life.

That's it.

(silence)

And then, you see, every time that Power of the new life comes, the whole body is thrown into a dreadful fright! Well, my FAN-TAS-TIC discovery *(Satprem pounds the ground with his fist)*, you see, my fantastic discovery is: WHAT IS AFRAID —IT'S DEATH THAT IS AFRAID!

It's death, inside the body, that is afraid—and tries to scare you to death and convince you: "You're dying, you're dying, you're dying. . . ."

It's death you are uprooting—not life. On the contrary, you're trying to bring in some real life.

That's it—that's it.

(silence)

When that Power comes down, there's a dreadful squirming in the body—mortal.

But the day I began to discover it was death that was afraid of dying, it was such a revelation for me, such a tremendous help. But this has to take place in the body, you understand. When your heart starts going "thump, thump" and gets stuck and . . . Well, afterwards, when it realizes—when it persists and realizes it didn't die, or when its brain is about to burst and it realizes it didn't burst. . . . But it takes many instances, you know, many such operations to uproot that falsehood, that fraud, that cruel domination. Because death is merely the end, but before getting there, you see all the horrors, the abominations, the suggestions: all that dominates, all that cruel squirming that dominates life *(pounding the ground)*, dominates men, dominates human consciousnesses—everything.

It's a CRUEL domination.

So the body must begin to realize that what dominates is the Lord, what dominates is Life, not death, that what is being uprooted from it is its old mortal rot—what is being uprooted is its old disaster.

I can assure you, that "stupid death," as Mother used to say—but it isn't stupid; it's nasty—that nasty death is saying, "Ah, you think I'm stupid!"

It's extremely clever, you know—it's clever day and night.

And very cruel.

But it's a FRAUD.

(Sri Aurobindo:) **Life and death are in fact one, and we may say from different points of view that all death is only a process and change of life**

or that all life is only an activity of death. Really both are one energy whose activity presents to us a duality of aspects. (16:359)

The Upanishads seized hold of the same truth when they declared life to be the dominion of King Death, described it as the opposite of immortality and even related that all life and existence here were first created by Death for his food. (16:338)

(Mother:) There can be no victory unless death is conquered. Death must be overcome; there must be no more death. This is very clear. (9/8/65)

Life Without Death

(Satprem continues:) That transitional being is one who is WITHOUT DEATH—it doesn't mean "immortal" as simplistic people think: one "regains youth" and all that nonsense. In fact, I don't know how it will be—I don't want to speculate—but it will be PURE life. That is to say, a life in which there is no death as at present, completely intertwined with life like a snake.

It will be PURE life: life without death.

It doesn't mean "immortal"; it means without death. There, death does not exist—death and ALL its tricks. Because death is just the end result, the culmination of meanness, deceit, cruelty, falsehood, perversity—of everything we see everywhere around us.

We see it "outside," but when you go inside yourself and you see DECEIT, MEANNESS, CRUELTY—and you realize how deeply ingrained all that filth is!

Death is nothing but the outcome of that.

That's exactly what Sri Aurobindo said: It's a "SPELL."[1] We must destroy that spell. The body must break through that spell. Only ABSOLUTE PURITY can break through.

So I think that's what the transitional being is: it means trying to uproot that filth, somehow. . . .

(Mother:) **There's a difference between immortality and the state without death. Sri Aurobindo explained it very well in Savitri.**

The state without death is what we can envision in the future for the human physical body: it is constant rebirth. Instead of slipping back and disintegrating for want of plasticity and from incapacity to adjust to the universal movement, the body is broken up in a forward movement, as it were.

There is an element that remains constant: in each type of atom, the inner arrangement of the elements is different, and that's what makes the difference in the substance. In the same way, maybe each person has a different and particular way of arranging the cells of his body, and that particular way is what persists throughout every outer change; everything else is broken up and rebuilt—but broken up in a forward move-

---

1. A spell is laid upon [our] glorious strengths (29:371)

ment instead of sinking backward into death, and rebuilt in a constant aspiration to follow the progressive movement of the divine Truth. (11/25/59)

What lives, what rules, what dominates, what is true, what is ONE, is . . . the Divine, is Mother—that's what exists, you understand. While everything else wants you to believe that falsehood is what exists.

We are *filled* with that mortal squirming, everywhere, in everything—snakes and claws, venom and suggestions—oh, it's . . . I don't know, we're full of it!

(silence)

That's the BASE: a life without death, a *pure* life, a life . . . freed from the fraud, from the illusion, from the MAGIC of death. That's the base. We have to build that base. Mother, Sri Aurobindo have built it, but a few bodies have to be willing to . . . follow!

What will happen after that base is established does not preoccupy me, I must say. But what is clear is that this *(Satprem strikes the ground several times with the palm of his hand)* is done—all the rest is divine play.

So you spend your time dying without dying.

The New Power

The body needs a good dose of it to begin . . . to feel differently.

For instance, the other day I truly thought I was going to die. My heart was really in a bad way. And I was in real pain. . . . But the body was not *in the least* worried—just the same it spent the day lying flat on the bed, but not in the least worried. It was just in pain. The next day, it wasn't at all over. I sat up and . . . that tremendous Power came, and the heart started to have, you know, those irregular heartbeats, which are kind of frightening for a body (!) Because when that Power comes, you feel as if it were going to crush everything—and what's a poor human heart compared to that!

Well, that was the breakthrough: the body took the resolution to say, "But dammit, is this the divine power or what! Is it the divine power that's trying to kill me? Good, if it wants to kill me, let it kill me!"

That was the body's reaction.

I stayed for, I don't know, an hour and a half, two hours, under that . . . Cataract (I don't know what else to call it; it's a Niagara of power, it's fantastic). And the body simply didn't concern itself with those . . . fluttering heartbeats. Everything went perfectly well for—after an hour and a half, I was a little tired, so I went and lay down. But everything went very smoothly. There was nothing wrong with me. On the contrary, it was going through like a breeze, a breeze, a breeze . . . And it *is* like a breeze! You see, what creates the explosion is all the falsehood and death swelling up and saying, "No, no, no, no, no, no, no. . . ."

(*Mother:*) I've noticed that if I resist, it gets worse. If I make myself fluid, there's no more friction. . . . If you tense up and things resist, nat-

urally you are going to get hurt. It's like people who know how to fall: they fall and don't break anything. But those who don't know how to fall, the least little fall and they pull something. It's the same thing. We must learn to be ... perfect oneness. To correct, to straighten is still to resist. (1/11/67)

What is not receptive feels the pressure, but what is receptive feels, on the contrary, a sort of ... powerful expansion. (5/6/72)

I had the same experience the other day. I had a racking headache, a real misery in my head (you know how it is, don't you?), and that same Power came. I said to myself, "It's going to break everything, shatter everything to pieces—it isn't possible. . . ." I stayed very quiet. But then, that same TREMENDOUS power is . . . it's like a breeze, a breeze, a breeze. . . .

(silence)

It's death that swells up, tenses and starts . . . going into hysterics—it wants you to believe that you are going to burst, that everything is going to burst.

But, of course, that kind of "operation" has to go on for several months, you understand.

(Luc:) But what does that Power *do* exactly? What is its .. function?

(Satprem:) Look, how do you go down into a body? When you want to dig a hole in something, what power do you use for digging? How would you dig in there without that power?

If you use your mind, it's like looking at all this with a little flashlight—which merely reflects on the surface. In order to go deeper, you literally need to *dig* in there, in those layers. The rishis said it: they said "digging." What are you going to "dig" with? What power? Your mental power? Even the power of your soul? Or your vital power? What can penetrate there? Only that other Power has the FORCE to penetrate there. But the moment it penetrates, it stirs up all the death that's in there!

Do you understand?

The first step, of course, is to establish a contact with that Power. Afterwards, well, it does its job—some job! . . . It's not you who do the job; all you have to do is try not to be party to that . . . mortal squirming. You mustn't be party to it—that's the difficulty.

We mustn't be party to it.

And it tries to get you in every conceivable way, using every conceivable means. I need not go into details. . . .

Well, that's some "digging," I assure you.

(Mother:) **As a result of that intensity of aspiration [in the body], I have a very clear and almost constant perception of the extent to which the material substance is made of falsehood and ignorance. As soon as the consciousness is quiet, at peace, in the luminous vision, it's as if all the falsehood came from everywhere. It isn't an active perception in the sense that I do not "try" to**

see: things come spontaneously before the consciousness. And you realize what tremendous power of Truth-Energy is necessary to clear up and transform all that! (2/26/64)

The Spell

Oh, now I understand the "process"—well, I listened to Mother for so many years, and of course I "understood" with my head, but now I understand with my *body*. I can assure you, it's one thing to see the fraud in your head and something else to see it in your body—to become aware of the *roots* of that cruelty. Oh, it's abominable!

(Sri Aurobindo:)
On dim confines where Life and Matter meet
... a weird and pigmy world
Where this unhappy magic had its source. (28:136)

Humans do not realize.

On the contrary, they spin, they endlessly spin all possible threads so as to be bound hand and foot by death. They spin them in every way: with their newspapers, their television, their science, their books, their novels, their adventures, their ... They spin ... truly, they SPIN death around them for the sake of spinning—they spin and spin endlessly. So afterwards, when you want to undo all that ... you must ask yourself, "My God, but what are they doing! *What* are they doing?"

137

Because all the means they use are PART of death! They are all the TRICKS of death: their surgery, their medicine, their physics, their science—they are all the tricks of death, the inventions of death, tricks to tie you up even more tightly.

Even their cures are part of death!

And they have frightful reasons on their side: "You see, you're going to die of this." They have certainty on their side, countless proofs—death is FULL of proofs. And you are absolutely under its control: even if you have some faith in your heart and your head, come a crucial moment, well, you're scared out of your wits and you go to the phone and call the doctor. And then go and acknowledge that you are wrong; then go and try to convince your body: "Look, this is not what you think!"

But they go on spinning and spinning, regardless. And so the world is in a colossal, dreadful spider web—which they spin foolishly, you see, day after day, with all their "things": their television, their newspapers, their novels, their literature, their poetry, their philosophy. Everything is an ENORMOUS spider web.

(long silence)

Six or seven months ago, I don't know, when for the first time I suddenly realized—but realized in my body, you understand—that it's death that is afraid of dying, it was such a . . .

It's DEATH that's afraid of dying.

Yes, I remember exactly.

And that's where you understand, you realize that Mother and Sri Aurobindo have seen all, said all, realized all. But to realize it in your mind isn't enough. I recall that phrase of Sri Aurobindo where he speaks of the "deep falsity of Death." The deep falsity of Death—well, it's "deep" within the body's tissues! That's where it's *deep*. But it's FALSE. It is a FRAUD. It is a LIE—a lie with millions of proofs on its side.

It is a lie.

The deep falsity of Death. . . .

You see, Sri Aurobindo often speaks of this "magic spell" or this "deformation spell" (at least four or five times in *Savitri*—it had struck me each time). "Spell"—he repeats the word three or four times in *Savitri*.

Well, that's what it is. It's really a "spell."

(Sri Aurobindo:)
Although God made the world for his delight,
An ignorant Power took charge and seemed his
Will
And Death's deep falsity has mastered Life.
(29:629)

The body's tissues thrill apotheosised,
Its cells sustain bright metamorphosis . . .
As if reversing a deformation spell (28:171)

(Mother:) Death isn't something inevitable; it's an accident that has always happened up until now—at least it seems to have always happened —and we have got it into our head and will to conquer and overcome that accident. But this is such a terrible battle, so gigantic, against all the laws of Nature, all the collective suggestions, all the terrestrial habits that, unless you are totally

fearless and a first-class warrior, you had better not begin the battle. You need to be an absolutely dauntless hero, because at every step and every second you have to do battle against everything that is established. So it isn't easy. And even individually, you have to fight with yourself, because, if you want your physical consciousness to be in a state that permits physical immortality, you must be free of everything that the physical consciousness now stands for. So it's a struggle at every second. All the feelings, all the sensations, all the thoughts, the reflexes, the attractions and repulsions, all that exists and makes up the very fabric of our physical life must be overcome, transformed and freed from all its habits. That means struggling every second of the day against thousands and millions of adversaries. (10/14/53)

In other words, the "divine life" begins when you can uproot that fraud, when you can create a base of pure life. Then the divine life begins—anyway, the one that... I don't know, I don't see it yet, but it will come. But this is not some philosophical divine life! It's a very... material divine life.

I have been talking a lot. . . .

(Satprem gets up)

And all their DNA molecules—that's still a view from inside the prison.

The New Being

(We resumed our walk. Satprem's words had made such a profound impact on me. I imagined his battle against the dark and demonic forces he had just described. Everything seemed so simple and obvious: we just had to go down into our body and kill the dragon dwelling there, the death snugly ensconced in our tissues, and we would be free at last on a true, happy and harmonious earth. I was walking beside him and our footsteps had a strange echo on that country road; they seemed to go deeper than the surface, almost as if they touched and pressed upon another dimension—perhaps a little bit upon the dragon's tail?

A few days earlier, a mutual friend had told us of a dream in which she had seen at length, and even talked to, a marvelous being, a child, of a different constitution from earthly beings, yet with a form very close to that of humans. That dream, and what was evoked by it, had very much struck Satprem.)

(Luc:) And what about that "new being" that S. saw in her dream?

(Satprem:) That's the future, the supramental being, the being who in fact is no longer made of all that mortal fabric of falsehood. It's a being who is made . . . divinely.

(Luc:) Could one say that the work you are doing is—

(Satprem:) You know, I wouldn't say "I" am doing, because you really have a feeling that the "I" is precisely what creates the obstruction—rather, you try not to stand in the way.

141

(Luc:) I understand. But is it conceivable that your endeavor brought that possibility faster, I mean, that child who seemed so close, so "concrete"? Could one say that in a sense he is born of—

(Satprem:) He is born of the supplications of some, and perhaps many, people who . . . Well, supplications. There are some good people on this earth, you know, who say to themselves, "My God, this isn't possible!" People who ache, you know. Well, there are ignorant supplications and others that are less ignorant. Without a doubt, every call has contributed. If there were nobody on this side to call for something truer, why should the Divine bother to do anything? He must be called, the Divine. . . . To call is in fact the first step toward liberation. There are no "individuals" in this— just calls. PURE calls. There may not be many, but there are some. There are beings who ache.

Sri Aurobindo and Mother sowed something, but on the other side there has to be . . . They threw her into the tomb, so there has to be a few people pure enough, with enough true love in their heart, to *call* her, to *draw* her out! Otherwise, why should she come out? She would stay forever in her tomb if people don't want her!

We must—we must call her.

And REALLY call her, you understand.

Not just as an idea.

It's SCALDING to be sincere; it's PAINFUL to be sincere.

So if this new being is . . . materialized, it's a marvelous grace. There's no other word for it. It's the solution to everything—if he's really materialized. Personally, I have seen him, but in a subtler world. Did he actually become material? It looks like it. I don't know, but for the last month or two, I have had such a strong feeling that something *had* to

142

happen. . . . It's possible—it isn't impossible. If he is here, it brings such a *tremendously positive energy* into the atmosphere—it's extraordinary! People can't understand, or else they understand through roundabout ways or masks. . . . It's bound to hasten everything toward the better, toward the True, and of course toward the collapse of Falsehood.
I don't know, my child.
We'll see—we'll see what happens.
I can only speak of my own experience: it's becoming very, very intense, very acute. One feels, I don't know, on the . . . brink of something.
Oh, yes! I understand Mother!—everything, absolutely *everything.* It's a pity I understand so late, because if I had understood her better then, I would have loved her a little more. That often makes me sad. . . .

(silence)

Well, anyway, my child, we'll see what happens. We must just do our part—let that white *laser* penetrate through all that squirming of falsehood. We must do our part, and that's all.

(Mother:) After speaking of the descent of the Supramental, he [Sri Aurobindo] said that we have to evolve an intermediate being between our present mental condition (even the most elevated mind) and the supramental region, because he said that if we entered the Gnosis directly, the change would be so abrupt that the constitution of our physical being would not be able to bear it—some intermediate being is nec-

143

essary. In view of what I have experienced, I am totally convinced of it: twice, there was an actual possession by the supramental world, and twice the body—the actual physical body—felt it was going to be completely disintegrated by ... what could almost be called the opposition of conditions. (10/15/61)

(Sri Aurobindo:) It is not to be supposed that all humanity would rise in a block into the supermind; at first those only might attain to the highest or some intermediate height of the ascent whose inner evolution has fitted them for so great a change or who are raised by the direct touch of the Divine into its perfect light and power and bliss. The large mass of humanity might still remain for long content with a normal or only a partially illumined and uplifted human nature. But this would be itself a sufficiently radical change and initial transformation of earth-life; for the way would be open to all who have the will to rise, the supramental influence of the truth-consciousness would touch the earth-life and influence even its untransformed mass and a hope would be there and a promise eventually available to all which now only the few can share in or realise. (16:22)

(Once again we sat under a tree. All human sounds seemed to have ceased. And again that same feeling of compact power near Satprem, at once gentle and imperative,

which seizes you from within.)

(Satprem, laughing:) They'll think he's an extraterrestrial!

> *(It took me a moment to come back to reality . . .)*

(Luc:) Ah, yes, that he came down from Venus!

(Satprem:) Oh, you know, their stupidity knows no limit! It knows no limit.

But I think that particular being will have . . . "powers"—but not the ones they think. Not the ones they think. He will burst the BUBBLE.

It's no use speculating. We know nothing—nothing. We know nothing.

The description [of the new being] that S. gave is ABSOLUTELY exact—and it's perfectly material.

Personally, I very much felt that something would happen—that something *had* to happen. That's all I can say.

> *(silence)*

Well, if he is here in matter, maybe his "radar" *(laughing)* will guide him to us, and he will come and say hello?

I did see something, but not in that form.

> *(silence)*

We are stuck inside a mortal fishbowl. We are like fish, hopelessly fish, and anything beyond the fishbowl is death-death-death-death—it's asphyxiation. Evidently, a few beings have tried to say, to show—to prove—that in fact one is not "asphyxiated"; one merely moves into another air, into a true life. And the whole "transition" is to try to poke one's nose outside of this human fishbowl. So if a first being quietly glides and slips to the surface, can you imagine what an extraordinary help that can be? A being who would be "supramental." If he is here, if he manifests himself . . . it will cause many things to collapse, it will help many things to collapse, many barriers. But, nonetheless, a few beings had to—have to—try to poke their nose to the surface, into the other air—which is NOT mortal.

(Sri Aurobindo:) **. . . Not only is death a seeming, but life itself is a seeming, and beyond life and death there lies a condition which is truer and therefore more permanent than either.** (12:1)

That is the true existence, the Life from which our life proceeds; that is the immortality, while what we cling to as life is "hunger that is death." (12:204)

(Mother:) **There's still a colossal work for everything to be transformed. But when you are on what could be called "the other side" (there are no "sides," but . . .), in the other state, it looks so natural, so simple, that you wonder why things aren't that way, why it is so difficult. And the moment you are back on this side, it's . . .** *(Mother takes her head between her hands).* **Clearly, there's still some mixture.**
Truly, the ordinary state, the old state, is conscious death and suffering (I mean, I have a con-

**scious perception of that). While in the other
state, death and suffering seem to be totally unreal.** (10/18/69)

The Cry

*(To my surprise, the next day Satprem asked me again to
bring the tape recorder on our walk. I felt encouraged to ask
the question I had been reluctant to ask.)*

(Luc:) I wanted to ask you a question about that "power"
you spoke of yesterday. From the outside, one gets the impression that it is rather as if a car were moving at a certain
speed, and accelerated and accelerated—and suddenly
there's a sort of break in the movement of the car: it leaves
the road and takes off into the air—it behaves in an altogether "unclassical" manner. As if that "power" had nothing
in common with our usual notion of spirituality.

(Satprem:) But of course, it has nothing in common!
They would be crushed to a pulp if they were in contact
with that!
The rishis, yes, *they* knew. . . .

(Luc:) So my question is to know how—not how one *gets*
it (I understand one doesn't "get" it; it has to come by itself),
but—

(Satprem:) What helps to make it come?

(Luc:) Yes . . . what has to happen, at some point, in the
being—in the body—for that Thing to manifest?

147

(Satprem:) All right, let me put things as simply as possible (I always use the same metaphor because I find it very vivid): we are REALLY like fish inside a fishbowl—it's an absolute fact. It is a fishbowl of *horror*, of *pain*, of *calamity*. But then ... (after all, sometimes there is a grace in life), all of a sudden, something in the body cries out ... CRIES OUT—something cries out materially, not in the mind, not as a result of self-discipline or anything of the sort. A cry suddenly bursts out of the ordinary man in the street because he is SUFFOCATING. And all of a sudden ... the fish sticks its nose out on the other side of the water, into another air—which is formidable (formidable, because he's still a fish). But, you see, you stick your nose out on the other side, you emerge—it's your SUBSTANCE that has to emerge there, nothing else! I'm talking of the cry of the man who is condemned to death, the cry of the man who is being tortured, the cry of the nightmare, the cry of—you've reached the END, you understand; you simply can't go on: you're dying.

So what is the way to get there? The way is uncatchable, indescribable; it belongs to no system, no spirituality, no ...—it belongs to the substance that CRIES OUT.

That cries out.

All of a sudden, in the middle of its nightmare, it cries out. In the midst of its pain, of its ... it lets slip a cry.

And you emerge a first time. You emerge ... and you are in that other Power of life—which is Life.

☆
☆ ☆

(Sri Aurobindo:)
All the world is changed to a single oneness
(5:563)

148

A Revolution in the Body

But the most extraordinary discovery that I—in my body, you understand, because you can discover anything you want in your head, it's just hot air; whereas when the body makes a discovery, it's . . . absolute, you know. It's like: suddenly it knows how to swim, or suddenly it knows how to— it KNOWS. These are absolute discoveries. Well, it was extraordinary that day when the body suddenly REALIZED (it was feeling all the horror of that cruelty, that suffering, that . . .), when it said to itself, "WHY, THIS ISN'T LIFE DYING; THIS IS DEATH LIVING!"

Do you understand?

It is DEATH that lives—it isn't life that dies; it's DEATH that lives.

I felt that death everywhere—death-death-death, cruel death. Death in every way: in my mind, my heart, my life. There was nothing but death and horror, really—what kind of life is this, for God's sake!

What kind of life is this?

And then—I don't know how to describe it, because for the body it's quite simple and overwhelming, like a complete reversal of all its values, but not "intellectual values"—suddenly it was right there in the flesh; it was . . . it was like being born to the world! Or being born to *a* world.

That's it: it isn't life that . . . ; it's DEATH that lives.

It created a sort of . . . revolution in the body, a complete reversal, a real breakthrough, I assure you.

There isn't any method.

You see, it is right at the *point* of dying that you begin to emerge. "At the point of dying"—you can die in your heart, die in your mind, die in your . . . in fact, we never stop dying in this life; that's all we do! But it has to become sufficiently

... that death has to hold you sufficiently in its grip ... so that there is such an intense aspiration in the body, you see—as when it is asphyxiated.

As when it is asphyxiated.

Well, look, there isn't any manual for that! You must ... all of a sudden you kick the bottom of that ... that hell, and you emerge. But "emerge"—it's in your SUBSTANCE that you eɹ.erge, not in your head, you understand! It is both EX-TREMELY SIMPLE and absolutely indescribable. There is no "path"; it's something completely automatic. There is no literature about it. There is no philosophy on it.

For the body, the Divine is something one DRINKS.

(Mother:) **And it isn't the result of an aspiration or research, an effort or a tapasya [discipline], nothing of the kind—it comes: plop!**

... And there is no imitating it. What's wonderful is that it can't be imitated! Everything else— for example, all ascetic realizations—can be imitated. But that cannot be imitated, because ... there's no equivalent anywhere.

... All your aspiration, your tapasya, your effort, all that is individual—absolutely no effect. It comes, and that's it.

You can do only one thing, which is to ANNUL YOURSELF AS MUCH AS POSSIBLE. If you can annul yourself completely, the experience is total. And if one could keep that blank state constantly, then the experience would remain there constantly. (2/25/61)

I tell you, the first time, it was—oh, it was like drinking nectar! The body was *drinking*. It drank for HOURS—it drank and drank and drank and drank.

I had never seen anything like it!

It was . . . it was unbelievable! It drank and drank and drank and drank—really as if it had been thirsty for thousands of years, and suddenly it was DRINKING the Divine! There was not even such a word as "divine"; it was just life pouring in for the first time.

(Sri Aurobindo:)
I have drunk the Infinite like a giant's wine.
(5:161)

So that Power is . . .

You can't describe the way—it's automatic. You can't "understand" it; you can't understand a way that doesn't exist—it is made *for you*. You can't "understand" it, because how can you ask a fish to understand what happens in the sunlight? It's impossible—it's another . . . way of being.

So it's automatic.

The only thing is the beginning: "Really, it's hell in here!" It's hell, and that's all. And it isn't just hell in your head—you're at the end of your rope! Then, all this matter, all that is covered up, you know, ENTOMBED, shut in a tomb—all this body covered up by that *dreadful* mental formation: that philosophy, religion, atavism . . . (the body is almost literally in a TOMB beneath all that!)—all of a sudden, all that breaks open.

The body suffocates!—we are just not aware of it. We notice it ... we notice it when it begins to die! But there's obviously no manual on suffocation or asphyxiation—at that moment whatever must happen happens. ...

Then, gradually—and that's the painful part—the old fish learns how to live in that other air, that other Power, that other kind of breathing.

But it is as material as this *(Satprem makes a fist)*. It's really—it isn't a metaphor—that material. One day, when the first fish became amphibian, it must have gone through hell—it must have been *asphyxiated* and *suffocated* in order to invent a new way of breathing. Well, this is exactly the same thing, you see.

It's EXACTLY the same—MATERIALLY the same.

These are not "metaphors."

The Other Air

I can tell you quite simply how it happened, the first time when really ... when it happened. I don't need to tell you all the details: truly, since the age of twenty I have been thrown into horror, and I did go through a lot of horror and pain and—a lot, a lot. ...

Anyway ...

(silence)

But a time comes when you really reach the end of the line. To reach it at twenty is already difficult; to reach it at sixty is in a way easier—but it's also more difficult. So there's really that ... burning NEED in the body—because all spiritualities and ideas and methods and all that are part of the fishbowl, part of the asphyxiation, part of the NOTH-

ING, you see. And then there's this matter, this body, so full of pain—and genuine pain, you know, because one has lived enough to be able to feel a little of all that misery, which is not only one's own, but the misery of this dreadful world. So you say to yourself, "That's it, you're going to die, and then what? What will you have DONE? What will you have truly LIVED? What is—WHERE IS LIFE, for God's sake?! Where *is* life?"

Where is life?

Well, one of these times (you can't pinpoint one in particular; there are millions of times, thousands of times, and some days it's more vivid than others—well, that day it was more vivid), it's absolutely as if everything in the body, all this consciousness, this . . . (this what? What drives this body), all this were seized with such an intensity—a MORTAL intensity, I could say—with such a CRY . . . I could see the entire course from the time I was twenty, with the Gestapo, till I was sixty—and what I saw was forty years of horror! FORTY years, you understand: I am sixty and I still find the SAME HORROR!

Truly, one can't talk about those things. . . .

So it's . . . I don't know. Of course, that cry happened many times before—many, many times, I am sure, and since very long ago.

But there was a day when all that cry of the body was like millions and billions of material particles, which started to rise and rise and rise and rise from the whole body. . . . So I said to myself, "This is it, you're going to die." And I couldn't have cared less. It was really like millions of particles of my body which . . . (were they the consciousness of my body? or the cry of my body? or what?—I can't say). But there was really the feeling of countless tiny particles leaving the body. As if the whole body were being emptied, you know—being emptied of all its being, of all its . . . life (or blood?).

And all of a sudden, it found itself . . . well, it found itself in that other air. . . . It had the impression of rising and rising and rising (while, in fact, it stayed right on the ground), and then it emerged into . . . into another air, another Power, another—call it what you like.

You can't describe these things. I tell you, it is both extremely simple and . . . People have to experience it, that's all.

People have to experience it.

(Sri Aurobindo:)
**A divine force shall flow through tissue and cell
And take the charge of breath and speech and**
act
**And all the thoughts shall be a glow of suns
And every feeling a celestial thrill.
Often a lustrous inner dawn shall come
Lighting the chambers of the slumbering mind;
A sudden bliss shall run through every limb
And Nature with a mightier Presence fill.
Thus shall the earth open to divinity
And common natures feel the wide uplift,
Illumine common acts with the Spirit's ray
And meet the deity in common things.
Nature shall live to manifest secret God,
The Spirit shall take up the human play,
This earthly life become the life divine.** (29:710)

(Mother:) It's a state, a state of intense vibration where you have at once a feeling of omnipotence, even in this *(Mother pinches the skin of her hand),* in this old thing, and ... a luminous omnipotence. And always with something comparable to goodness, benevolence, but far beyond those things (they seem like ridiculous distortions in comparison). This *(gesture of expansion)* and static at the same time. In other words, there's a feeling of eternity in the cells. (4/23/69)

There must be enough of a CRY, enough intensity of call, enough ... This is perhaps how all mutations happened? Because a given species is dying—well, it's got to find the other way, or perish.

This is what has to happen in a few individuals.

And it can be ANY individual.

The grace is ... to call.

That's all.

We could also say that the grace is to asphyxiate....

That's true.

And, of course, this has nothing to do with any spirituality. You see, I did do ... well, I've had all sorts of experiences in my life. So as far as the regions "above" are concerned, the super-regions of yogis and people who practice meditation, I know them well—I've explored them. Well, I tell you, they seem like a *paltry* dream in comparison—like a dream. That power has such a DENSITY! And yet, it is such an incredible nectar. It's something you TASTE, you DRINK, you ... INHALE. How can you possibly describe that? For the body, which has been living in death for . . . well, for nearly sixty years in my case (and for each person, it's been death for as long as he or she has lived), all of a sudden, it's life!

All of a sudden, it's life!

But it's a life that . . . You do not emerge into it once and for all, you see. You carry with you all the old fish. So you must constantly . . . well, now the old fish must learn the new way of breathing, the new way of being. It must be learned. And learned how? Well, learned by asphyxiating, by painful labor, by—you learn it on the job. This is not in any manual, you see. And then, it will vary; it will be different for each individual. How do you learn to evolve from fish to amphibian? How do you learn to grow legs to walk on the ground? Yes, how do you learn? . . .

That's it, you see.

The fins have to change into something that can walk, the lungs have to change into something that can breathe the air—it's a completely new way of being. It has to be developed, to be learned. . . .

(Mother:) **It can't last, mostly because of the constant contact with . . .** *(gesture showing the old world around Mother)*. **But even without that contact, for example at night, it may stay an hour, two hours, in that state, and suddenly, you don't know why, it slips back into the other way. And you hurt here, hurt there; you're uncomfortable, oh . . . terrible.** (4/9/69)

An Automatic Path

Well, there isn't any manual for that. There's nothing.

It's a wonderful path (in a sense), because, since you can't know ANYTHING about it, you're certain not to make any mistakes! You are certain. You *can't* make any mistakes. Because you can't know what the next step should or shouldn't be—you simply can't. You don't know—you know NOTHING! What does a fish know about life in the sunshine? It knows NOTHING.

So it's a totally automatic path—totally material and totally automatic. You meet all the obstacles, all the difficulties, all the complications—all that is necessary for you to learn the new way of breathing, the new way of walking, the new way of being. And you can't invent it; you can't plan it—it's impossible. Impossible.

You can't make any mistakes—there is no road!

(Mother:) **No more ties—free, free, free, free! Always ready to change everything, except one thing: aspiration, that thirst. (10/7/64)**

I don't know what's going to happen—the body is not told what will happen. Actually, it's easy to understand: if the body knew in advance what will happen, it would probably do something stupid instead of being very attentive and very ... well, receptive, not just "listening" (it isn't just a matter of hearing something), but attentive to the Impulse, to do exactly what must be done—what is expected of it—for everything,

absolutely everything, down to the least detail: eating, sleeping, speaking, moving, everything. To be like that all the time, all the time: attentive to do nothing except what has to be done. (6/25/69)

And, you know, if you tried to deceive yourself—pfft! *(gesture of a blade across the throat)* It's impossible, you see, because it is overwhelming. It is, in fact, a PURE air, so if the least thing is impure, it's . . . simply pulverized. And that's not a joke! You must be TOTALLY pure—in fact, the whole task is for the old fish to purify itself of all its old . . . way of being. And if you try to bring a little of the fish into the other air, it EXPLODES! You can't cheat with "that," you see. You simply can't; it's impossible—it's a material fact. You can't bring any of the fish to the other side; it's impossible.

I could say any fool can do it. But it has to be a fool who is really asphyxiating, really crying out, really calling, really . . .

All those who believe they have remedies, panaceas, tricks are still *completely* stuck in the death of the fishbowl—they are nothing but panaceas of death. The point is, you must be at the end of all "panaceas"—at the end of everything.

(Mother:) It's day after day, you know, with something new every day; and always the same immediate conclusion: I know nothing, I understand nothing, I am nothing. . . . The negation of EVERYTHING. All the mental props of the human

consciousness are gone. And for little things, for big things—for everything. (5/10/69)

If Sri Aurobindo and Mother had not MADE the way, it would be completely impossible, you know, because . . . you would panic instantly. It would be impossible—they had to open the way because you would think you've gone insane. You'd fall directly into death!

So the way has been opened.

In other words, the surface of that . . . mortal illusion has been BROKEN. And through that break, let's say that . . . others, in turn, can pass: their cry can get through.

(Mother:) **It must be "worked out," as they say; it must be worked out in detail, but the change is accomplished—the change IS ACCOMPLISHED.**

That is, the material conditions that have been elaborated by the mind, fixed by it *(Mother closes her fist tightly)*, and which seemed so inevitable—to the point that those who had a living experience of the higher worlds thought it necessary to escape this material world, abandon it, in order really to live the Truth (that's the origin of all those theories and beliefs)—but now it's no longer the case! Now it's no longer the case. The physical is capable of receiving the higher Light, the Truth, the true Consciousness, and of MANIFESTING it.

It isn't easy; it requires endurance and will-power, but a day will come when it will be totally

natural. The door is just ajar—and now we have to walk through it. (3/14/70)

That's the difficult part, but it's also a marvel—a lived marvel. But you can't talk about these things. It's like discovering life, you see!

It's truly like that.

The Delight in the Body

I didn't realize. . . . Once, I had to go to F. to the dentist, and I felt really miserable, as if I were at the end of my life. I felt so . . . exhausted by all those people rushing and bustling about. And I did not realize how much of that other air I had already absorbed (you don't realize that you absorb a lot, a lot of that other air). I came back home—and suddenly what an incredible TORRENT OF LIFE came pouring in! I drank it, drank it as if my body . . . It was fabulous! The body, these billions of cells were all drinking and drinking and drinking and drinking as if . . . I can't say. It's . . . it's concrete!

It's truly a nectar. It's something that has never been experienced.

So, for the body, it's divine—it *is* the Divine. It's adorable, delightful; it's a delight. No words are necessary—but the body understands! It understands.

(Sri Aurobindo:)
It is Thy rapture flaming through my nerves

160

And all my cells and atoms thrill with Thee;
My body Thy vessel is and only serves
As a living wine-cup of Thy ecstasy. (5:135)

You can't imagine how marvelous it is. . . . It's really as
if this body—this body, these cells—had lived for thousands
and thousands of years, gone through desert after desert
after desert, and suddenly it finds the *water* of life—a water
it never knew, an air it never knew, which is its first breath
ever. It's unbelievable, I assure you. It's unbelievable! It isn't
expressible—it's a fact. You can't compare it with anything.

And that is life!

That is life. A life that will . . . build everything, that will
make Life!—which has never been, you see.

Which has never been. . . .

We'll see what the future has in store—that doesn't preoccupy me.

(silence)

That swelling of delight in the body! . . . It's unbelievable,
inexpressible!

It's a complete revolution, a trauma in reverse. I don't
know how to describe it: it was dead and now it is living!
How can you express that? And even trying to express it
is . . .

Yes.

(Sri Aurobindo:)
All my cells thrill swept by a surge of splendour.
Rigid, stone-like, fixed like a hill or statue,

161

Vast my body feels and upbears the world's
weight;
Dire the large descent of the Godhead enters
Limbs that are mortal. (5:53)

(Mother:) **When the new way comes in pure, un-**
mixed, the body, the consciousness of the body,
still has that reaction of . . . *(Mother makes a*
movement of surprise) **wonder at something that**
still seems impossible. (4/4/70)

But that, it doesn't forget—it doesn't forget. That leaves a marvelous imprint everywhere, in its myriad cells. From that moment on, it—that's what helps, what will help it to undergo that purification (indeed painful) of everything that's left of the old fish, you see. That's the tough part: that old death that still sticks to you, yes *(laughing)*, the remains . . . of the old fish, which must still be purified.

But it leaves such an imprint . . . I don't know.

It's like a collapse in reverse. I can't tell you: It was dead and now it is living; it was locked in a prison of all sorts of things, and pfft, the prison is gone! You have to breathe that to . . . all of sudden to appreciate the sort of CATACLYSM it creates in that squirming—but a wonderful cataclysm! It's a reversal of everything: there was death, and now there's life (while the body thought there was life when there was, in fact, death). Everything is reversed. And not in the HEAD—the body has UNDERSTOOD.

It has understood forever.

(silence)

Come, let's walk a little. . . .

(Mother:) **Mentally, you can explain everything, but it means absolutely nothing. For the body, for the material consciousness, it's an abstraction. Once the material consciousness has grasped something, it knows it a hundred times better than we can know something through mental knowledge. When it knows, it acquires the power to do—that gives the power to do.** (3/13/68)

Before—long ago, many years ago—whenever I had an experience, it was the mind that more or less benefited from it, then spread it around and used it. Now it's no longer that way: it's the body directly; it's the body that has the experience, and it is much truer. There's a certain intellectual attitude that puts a sort of veil or some ... I don't know, something, something unreal over our perception of things—it's an attitude, just an attitude. It's as if you were looking through a veil or a ... something, a certain atmosphere. Whereas the body feels the thing in itself—it BECOMES it. (7/25/70)

A World Simply True

(We resumed our walk. All the trees around us stood out with amazing clarity on the horizon. Satprem continued:)

And so they all spend their time worshiping the tomb of Mother and Sri Aurobindo—instead of making a HOLE in it!

(silence)

They are the ones who are entombed.

(silence)

It will be so beautiful the day when that tomb of the world, that tomb of pain and falsehood and horror BREAKS OPEN, when a new earth comes into being at last, into the open air, into a delightful air, a true air, yes, really true....

It's a TRUE world, you know! *(in a sobbing voice)* It's ... TRUE. For once, it's true, simply true.

(silence)

Perhaps the blessing of our times, of our century, of our ... (the blessing of our horror, one could say) is that we have reached such a horrible point that ... things will break and we'll emerge into something else. Not break with their bombs—that's still the triumph of the old death—but something that breaks in the human consciousness. This is perhaps the blessing of this horrible age. Before, the Horror had a lovely mask: it had beautiful literature, beautiful religion, beautiful spirituality. Everything was gilded and respectable—now it's stark naked. That, too, is a blessing. You can no longer be deceived. There's a whole illusion that nobody can entertain anymore; all that is finished. These are moments of grace, precisely because the illusion is for the most part shattered.

(silence)

Shall we sit a little?

*(We sat at the edge of a field,
beneath a beautiful tree with
a smooth, straight trunk.)*

164

(Luc:) The trouble is that in this world—in society, let's say—if a man had such an experience, if his cry succeeded in tearing the veil, in breaking the fishbowl, he would instantly think he'd gone crazy!

(Satprem:) You must never forget that that "other thing" is truly divine: it's the pure Divine, the lived Divine. So it takes very great care of . . . whatever may happen. One could say that it automatically takes care of what's there. That's the whole point: it's "unthinkable," it's . . . an automatic, effortless, natural marvel. Completely natural: "it" does exactly what is needed, and "it" knows exactly everything there is to know.

Those who'd become crazy are those who would have cheated in one way or another.

It's measured—it has to be, I should think! If you emerged completely, entirely into it, well, there would probably be an explosion; everything would be shattered, pulverized. As far as I can tell, it comes in stages. In stages—that is, each time it's a deeper physical layer that is touched. Naturally, the deeper it is, the more powerful it is. . . . It's measured—there's no need of any description, of any system, because it's marvelously and automatically divine.

It is precisely the opposite of everything that happens in this phony, twisted mind, which is capable of taking the most marvelous spirituality and turning it into the most marvelous fakery—it's the OPPOSITE of that.

In a way, it's frightening, but it's frightening for the old death, for the old falsehood, for everything that's twisted.

That's what has to happen to everyone . . . just in the right "measure," in the right way, at the right moment.

Only death can die!

It's . . . really the truth.

Oh, you know, it's so extraordinarily simple!
Only falsehood can become crazy! Only what is twisted
can become twisted. . . . It's very simple!

(silence)

Someone, obviously, had to . . . open the passage for the
first time, because . . . Someone had to do it once. And that's
where the work done by Sri Aurobindo is fantastic, you
know—it's unbelievable.
It's unbelievable. . . .

☆
☆ ☆

(Sri Aurobindo:)
I have been digging deep and long
    Mid a horror of filth and mire
A bed for the golden river's song,
    A home for the deathless fire.
I have laboured and suffered in Matter's night
    To bring the fire to man;
But the hate of hell and human spite
    Are my meed since the world began. . . .
My gaping wounds are a thousand and one
    And the Titan kings assail, . . .
A voice cried, "Go where none has gone!
    Dig deeper, deeper yet
Till thou reach the grim foundation stone
    And knock at the keyless gate." . . .
[I] plunged through the body's alleys blind
    To the nether mysteries
I have delved through the dumb Earth's
                   dreadful heart
    And heard her black mass' bell.

I have seen the source whence her agonies part
And the inner reason of hell. (5:99)

Well, people, the world, are approaching that Moment.
We are approaching that moment of . . . the Marvel.

While, for them, it's a cataclysm, it's "death"—but everything is upside down! Everything is upside down! For them,
we are approaching a cataclysm, the end of God knows what,
of the world. But it continues. . . . It's certainly the end of
the fish . . . (that wouldn't be too bad!) or at least of this kind
of . . . intelligent fish.

We must dare!

(silence)

There are plenty of "manuals" on how to do Yoga—there's
no manual for being thirsty.

(silence)

And if you are thirsty, the river comes to you; if you are
not thirsty, the river does not exist.

It does not exist.

(silence)

The Marvel. . . .

One day, you know, it struck me—it struck me without
warning. It seized hold of me in such an . . . unbearable way.
I had just turned sixty, and one night I *again* found myself
with the Gestapo, in that world of horror. And I thought, "So
there it is: you've dragged that horror for *forty* years. You've
dragged that horror for FORTY years—and you're still drag-
ging it!"

167

It was . . . crushing, really. I was crushed with despair. I found myself again in that nightmare, in that perverse world, as only humans can invent perversity. And I thought, "This has been going on for FORTY years!"

I have had that nightmare thousands of times.

Well, the entire world is right in the nightmare.

(Sri Aurobindo:)
It was a space where nothing could be true, . . .
A vast deception was the law of things (28:206)

This is what you have to take back with you: That exists. There is that Marvel—IT EXISTS.

It isn't complicated.

It exists.

(silence)

We just have to realize it's there. . . .

(silence)

What is that Marvel going to do? What is that Power of pure life going to do? We don't know. There is no path—it just happens. We cannot "understand"—it just happens. We don't know how it works.

You see, sometimes, when that Marvel comes, it's like . . . I can't say, it's at once a Nectar and a torrent of FIRE, unbearable for all that is mortal, precisely. So if you put people face to face with a flood of FIRE and told them, "Well, go right ahead!"—they couldn't do it. And it's obvious: you *can't* do it. Well, all life is like that, with death saying: "You can't do it. You can't do it. Listen, be reasonable; you can't do it." It's

168

DEATH that makes all the you-can't-do-it, you-can't-do-it, you-can't-do-it. . . . And that's that—and mathematical to boot.

So it isn't in the *head* that you can do this. It must be experienced by the cells of our body! That "you-can't-do-it" must simply cease to exist for the cells! And then it will be over: no more "you-can't-do-it." Then everything will be possible.

(Mother:) **All the impossibilities, all the "it-cannot-be," "it-cannot-be-done"—all that is swept away. But it's swept away *in principle*, and it's trying to become a fact, a concrete fact.** (8/5/70)

So I don't imagine anything, I don't speculate about anything, but I know *that's how it is*: that some "you-can't-do-its" are clearing out, and all the "you-can't-do-its" will eventually clear out, and . . . we'll see what happens!

But the first and foremost magic wand of death is that "you-can't-do-it."

That's how it possesses us. And it's a magic wand that's "scientific" to boot!

But one can't undo the "spell" in one's mind. Only the BODY can undo its own spell. That's the *only* place where it can be undone, where you go from the fishbowl into the open air. It's your old fish matter that emerges—it's in matter that it can be done, that the spell can be undone, not in the brain. It may be good to know about it intellectually, but that's not where it takes place, you see. This is not a "liberation" up above in heaven—it takes place IN matter. And there, well, everyone's on his own. It just happens.

And sometimes it happens in spite of yourself and in an unexpected way! You can't do anything about it. All you can do is to cry, to . . . to do the work of a true human being, that is, a little sincere.

But the world that is coming is prodigious, you know! It is there, approaching . . . waiting for us—waiting for us to get out of this evil spell.

The thing is, you can't pretend anything, you can't invent anything; it's done FOR you. It is precisely a world in which there is no more "pretending," no more "cheating": it's the pure simplicity of Truth—I say "Truth," but it's still an abstract word; it's PURE simplicity, you see, like breathing air. You can't cheat. You can't "imagine things," you can't invent things—you can't pretend. There can be no counterfeiter, no fraud—it's the "Truth." It's PURE air. And if you try to cheat, you die instantly! Everything that's corrupted and mortal in you dies instantly.

(Mother:) **"What You will, as You will." Truly, you must have the concrete sensation that this [the body] does not exist—it's just as if "utilized"— and that there is ONLY THAT. That conscious immensity . . . *(Mother opens her arms wide)*, that IMMENSE Force, IMMENSE Vibration, which presses and presses and presses . . . and then the Thing opens up, and when it opens, that spreads out.**
This is the only solution. There's no other solution. All the rest is . . . aspirations, conceptions,

hopes—it's still the superman, but it isn't the supramental. It's higher humanity trying to lift its humanity upward, but ... it's useless. It doesn't work.

I have such a vivid image of all that humanity grappling to raise itself, trying to catch hold of something, but it doesn't give itself—it just wants to take! And that won't do. It must annul itself. Then something else can come and take its place.

That's the whole secret. (12/13/69)

What is absurd here is all the artificial means one must use. Any fool has more power if he has the means of acquiring the necessary contrivance. Whereas in the supramental world, the more conscious you are and in harmony with the truth of things, the more authority willpower has over matter. Authority is true authority. If you want clothes, you must have the power to make them, a genuine power. If you don't have that power, well, you go naked. There's no contrivance to make up for the lack of power. Here, not once in a million is authority the expression of something true. Everything is extraordinarily stupid. (2/58)

Well, it's going to be—it will be—an absolutely wonderful world, you know! Not in the sense that people think, but wonderfully simple—divinely simple! No more tricks. No more gimmicks. No more "Great Powers"—all those people

171

loaded with "Powers": the superyogis, superpresidents. . . .
No more powers—the only "power" is simply to breathe and
to be. No more "powers," you see—all that is over. These
"powers" are just the tricks of Falsehood: "Me, I am capable
of doing this and that!"

It's death that is "capable."

(silence)

Oh, how good it will feel the day when all the frauds of
the world CRUMBLE! It will feel so good!

(silence)

And in the meantime, they elect the next president—they
always elect the next liar. Or else they pick up the phone to
call the next liar who will help them . . . to die.

(silence)

I speak to you, brother, because you will be in that world.
Not "another" world—this one. You will be there—you will.
You are already in it. You still don't realize it completely,
because . . . you have a job to do, and in order to do that job
effectively, you still need to wear masks. . . .

It's temporary.

(long silence)

Mother is gracious, you know. . . . She is gracious. It takes
very little on our part—our poor part—it takes very little for
Her to . . . rush to the rescue and help.

We are very obtuse, you know. We are precisely doing our
old work of being obtuse.

(silence)

I think . . . everything is VERY CLOSE.

172

We have been created . . . for that Marvel . . . for that Delight . . . on earth.

(to be continued . . .)

BIOGRAPHICAL NOTES

SRI AUROBINDO was born on August 15, 1872, in Calcutta, India. At the tender age of seven, his father, a country doctor, sent him to England for "serious studies," as was the custom of the day among certain anglicized Indian families. For 13 years Sri Aurobindo would be immersed in Western culture—which would eventually reward his academic prowess with abundant laurels. In 1893, at the age of twenty, his Cambridge degree in his pocket, he returned to India to find a profoundly revolting political and social situation in his country (under British rule). After a few years spent between a teaching post of French and English at the College of Baroda and the private secreteriat of the local maharaja, Sri Aurobindo moved to Calcutta and entered the political fray. Simultaneously, he set out on his inner quest not to escape into higher worlds of consciousness, but as a means of sharpening his revolutionary action against the British occupation. As editor of the daily *Bande Mataram* (Hail to Mother India) and leader of the *Extremist Party*, he would soon be suspected of participating in a criminal attempt against a British magistrate, and he would spend a year in prison while awaiting trial. That year of forced isolation made him realize that the occupation of his country by a foreign power was but one aspect of a much vaster problem: the transformation of human nature. "It is not just a revolt against the British empire that we must wage, but a revolt against the whole universal Nature!" he exclaimed. Acquitted but still pursued and spied on by the British pol-

174

ice, he had to take refuge in French India, in Pondicherry, where he arrived in 1910. This is where he spent the rest of his life until 1950, in the "ashram" that gradually formed around him under the supervision of Mother, who joined him in 1920. His written work, mostly composed between 1914 and 1920, comprises poetry, plays, "philosophy" and an enormous body of letters to try to explain to his disciples what he was doing in the silence of his room.

It was while visiting Pondicherry in 1914 that MOTHER met Sri Aurobindo for the first time. She would come back and settle beside him in 1920, after a stay in Japan and a short visit to China. Mother was born in Paris in 1878 as Mirra Alfassa. As a young girl she already had strange experiences that took her into the past and perhaps into the future; she met Sri Aurobindo "in dream" ten years before meeting him physically in Pondicherry. Gifted in mathematics, music and painting, she befriended many of the great Impressionist painters of the time—Gustave Moreau, Rodin, Monet—and married a painter, whom she divorced to marry a philosopher, who took her on a trip to Pondicherry. She lived thirty years beside Sri Aurobindo, assuming the direction of his ashram and, after his departure in 1950, plunging herself into the "yoga of the cells" to open the "Great Passage" to the next species. For almost twenty years, from 1954 to 1973, she confided her intimate experiences and the unfolding of the physical process of transformation to Satprem, who alone was willing *materially* to believe in what she was doing. These conversations constitute *Mother's Agenda* in 13 volumes.

BIBLIOGRAPHY

All of Mother's quotations dated after 1953 are taken from *Mother's Agenda* in 13 volumes. A few quotations dated prior to 1953 are excerpted from *Questions and Answers*.

Sri Aurobindo's quotations are drawn from *The Centenary Edition*, which includes Sri Aurobindo's entire works in 30 volumes numbered from 1 to 30. The passages mentioned in this book refer in particular to the following volumes:

5 – *Collected Poems*
12 – *The Upanishads*
16 – *The Supramental Manifestation*
17 – *The Hour of God*
18 – *The Life Divine*, vol. 1
19 – *The Life Divine*, vol. 2
22 – *Letters on Yoga*, vol. 1
24 – *Letters on Yoga*, vol. 2
26 – *On Himself*
28 – *Savitri*, vol. 1
29 – *Savitri*, vol. 2

Further passages from the following books have been used:

31 – *Life of Sri Aurobindo*, by A.B. Purani
32 – *Correspondence with Sri Aurobindo*,
      by Nirodbaran
33 – *Evening Talks with Sri Aurobindo*,
      by A.B. Purani
34 – *Talks with Sri Aurobindo*,
      by Nirodbaran